PRAISE FOR "PERFECTLY REVOLTING"

"You will love Kristen Caven's book, *Perfectly Revolting,* if you:
a) ever attended an all-woman college.
b) are or ever have been a feminist.
c) are or ever have been a "women's libber."
d) are or ever have been a cartoonist.
e) are or ever have been a woman.
f) are or ever have been a man.
g) were born with a funnybone.
h) all of the above."

—*Trina Robbins, comics legend and author of* The Brinkley Girls,
From Girls to Grrlz, The Great Women Cartoonists, *and more*

"A great gift to the college.... what a wonderful way to document an important historical time for Mills."

—*Mandy Benson, Assistant Director of Student Activities, Mills College*

"That Kristen, she's one funny b****."

—*David Bryce, rock star*

PRAISE FOR THE 1990 STUDENT STRIKE

"My most glorious defeat. One of the most maturing experiences of my life."

—*Warren Hellman, a.k.a. "Warren Go-to-Hellman",* *see page 104*

Talk about a cartoonist?

Julie Graham

The big talk these days around the old college green is about the new Mills Weekly cartoonist. Who is that woman with the offbeat sense of humor, who makes us laugh over the Aliso Frog Choir or Sammy the Sperm's latest adventure? And why is she incognito?

Kristen Baumgardner is not exactly shy. Her latest public performance found her in the campus lip-sync contest mouthing Lois Armstrong's version of "Mac the Knife." However, Baumgardner prefers to keep a low profile in her new role as campus cartoonist.

"It's part of being on a small campus, she says. "We should take a look at what's around us, but satire is difficult. You have to think about who you might offend."

Her mother's career as a psychologist helped Baumgardner get an early start at cartooning. By providing art work for the pamphlets, booklets and brochures for her mother's workshops, she got a lot of practice.

Recently she has been working hard on illustrating her mother's first published book, *The Winning Family* by Dr. Louise Hart. "It was strange when I talked to the editor about the sample drawings I submitted," said Baumgardner. "She told me, 'We

Our glamorous cartoonist, Kristen Baumgardner

like your drawings very much but we don't think it will work with (your mother's) book. We want you to do another book'." Eventually, after she and her mother wrote a few more letters to the editor about her art, they succeeded in having the editor choose her work for the illustrations.

The hardest part about being the cartoonist for the college paper, she says, is having a commitment each week to come up with something funny.

"Mostly I look for things that amuse me. That's really the only criterion. Like the cartoon about the woman sticking her hands in Campbell's soup (see the March 13 issue). That came from when I was eating lunch with some friends and I stuck my fingers in my soup because they were cold. I guess I'm a pretty silly person so it all comes natural to me."

Baumgardner grew up in Boulder, Colorado. Since graduating from high school in 1982, she has attended St. John's College and the Rocky Mountain College of Art and Design. Here at Mills she is working toward a College Major, with an emphasis in literature. She would someday like to write and illustrate children's books.

Some of her idols include Gary Larson ("The Far Side"), Berke Breathed ("Bloom County") and Shel Silverstein ("Light in the Attic"). Baumgardner is drawn to satire and says that she would like to take her artistic license and run away with it because so few women cartoonists attempt satire.

But she adds, "Everyone is fair game for a cartoonist, and I'm finally going to have to decide not to take responsibility for everyone. People need to learn to laugh at themselves more."

Mills Weekly: February 12, 1987

glamourous cartoonist: <u>there's</u> an oxymoron!

Perfectly Revolting
My Glamorous Cartooning Career

Kristen Baumgardner Caven

Murray,
I guess I owe it
all to you!

This book is dedicated to girls who snort when they laugh
(and cry when they're upset).

ISBN-10: 1-4414-1543-2
ISBN-13: 978-1-4414-1543-1

10 9 8 7 6 5 4 3 2
First Edition

Oodles of thanks to Caitlin Ayers,
my minion from Mills,
who helped a whim become a work.

Introduction

The reason this book exists is because twenty years ago the board of directors at a college I happened to be attending decided to make a radical change. This change was NOT okay with the students, and they did something about it, something that made headlines around the globe: they cried. And then they shut the campus down.

The college was Mills, a small liberal arts school in Oakland, California. The year was 1990. And the issue was MEN. The board decided to admit men to Mills, a hundred-year-old educational institution for women.

I had graduated from Mills several years before this event, but like the other alumnae (yes, —ae is the correct Latin ending for a plural female noun), I wanted to support the hundreds of students who blockaded every doorway and kept faculty and staff away from their offices for fifteen days until they reversed the decision. I had been the campus cartoonist during my three semesters at Mills, and when I arrived on the scene, I did what came naturally: I drew. What the media saw as hysterical women, I saw as hysterical women. I visited blockades, listened to stories, and put all the funniest bits together in one place.

The resulting ten cartoons won an award in a local cartoon contest, and I published them in a thin volume which was banned from the campus bookstore the day it hit the shelves. I also printed t-shirts featuring the celebratory "Men of Mills College Pin-Up Calendar," which shows twelve months of blank pages.

When I got the idea to publish the twentieth-anniversary edition of *Inside the Mills Revolution: A Cartoon History of the Student Strike*, I decided to include a few of my campus cartoons that featured Mills. But once I started digging in my drawers (sorry, that sounds a little gross), I realized that the story of how I came to draw the student strike was a part of my own evolution as a cartoon artist—and a woman.

I've woven my story throughout the cartoons so you can join me on this journey, which begins when I came to Mills to complete my education and ends several years after my graduation. But you totally don't have to read it all. If you want to skip through and just read the cartoons, go for it. If you want to know a little back story, though, turn the page.

My inner child gets lots of exercise.

I came to California a confused young thing who was unsure of her role on this planet as a woman with a brain of her own, and in it, a questioning mind.

I had been born less than a year after my toy-stealing, fast-running, hard-hitting, but totally god-like big brother, becoming hard-wired from the moment I met him to pal around with, square off with, compare myself with, and compete with BOYS. In a fourth-grade fantasy of who I would be at age thirty, I dreamed of being an artist. I would live in the desert with one horse, two dogs, three cats, four gerbils, etc. etc. etc. (and a conspicuous absence of men). I would have long, straight, blonde hair down to my butt. I would wear a clingy blue bell-bottomed pantsuit with a round zipper pull.

My family is full of people with big ideas and very sensitive funny bones. When I got to high school, I loved philosophizing with my girlfriends more than anything. Anything except for maybe getting a laugh from my classmates. I started to draw cartoons. But I was characteristically annoyed by the fact that smart-ass boys tended to get more laughs and attention with their obnoxious and crude jokes than smart-ass girls with subtle wits. I loved these funny boys, but I couldn't be like them. To them, I was just a cute girl (one of many)—who was, well, just a little weirder than the others.

Being such a fan of philosophizing, I chose a liberal arts college that was specially designed for questioning and pondersome types. All of our classes were based on discussions of some Great Book or another. Sometimes, however, as an intuitive smart-ass, I would lose patience in all the logical deliberation, and want to "get to the punchline." My science professor, aware of my cute weirdness, worried about this tendency to "fall back on whimsy." But I took my whimsy very seriously, sensing that it might have the power to lead me to the destiny of my dreams.

One day I woke up and realized that all the Great Books I loved and loathed so well were written by Great Men who, when they mentioned women, tended to talk about them as if they were a separate species that alternated between being predatory and threatening—or stupid and inferior. By my junior year, I had worked up a serious identity crisis.

I decided to get back to my dream. I dropped out and enrolled in an art school close to home. I started

"Why, Liberal Arts, of course. What's your major?"

growing my hair long and wondered if polyester pantsuits would ever come back in style. I loved drawing and painting every day, and learned some tricks of the trade. But as much as art school nourished my soul, I missed the life of a contemplative intellectual. When the school asked me if I wanted to be a Fine Artist, a Graphic Artist, or an Illustrator I just said, "yes, please." Because, somewhere along the line, I had already committed myself to being a Liberal Artist:

- *Liberal*, as in free (Latin: *liber*) to do as I please.

- *Liberal*, as in plentiful (as in "a liberal helping of mashed potatoes.")

- And *Liberal*, as in relating to and being surrounded by books (Spanish: *libros*.)

Somehow I found my way to Mills College, a Liberal Arts school for women with a brand new Art building. There, I was finally able to confront the ideas, beliefs, and perceptions I'd formed about womanhood, a state towards which I seemed to be hurtling at an alarming speed.

Cartoonists are naturally rebellious by nature. Deep down, they're perpetual smart-ass adolescents. In editing this book, I became reacquainted with the part of myself that is shaped by these impulses, as well as my conflicting perfectionist impulses of being a female. Females (most of them at least) possess a survival instinct to keep their images refined and their actions beyond reproach. Writers and artists, on the other hand, have a passion to express themselves with emotional abandon, impolite wit, and apolitical accuracy. In curating my collected cartoons for this book, I observed myself in the process of figuring out what I—as a female, a wise guy, an artist, a philosopher, a writer, or whatever—was meant to be.

Meanwhile, to get back at my inner child for the cartoonish image of myself as a "glamorous" adult, here is a version of myself as that sincere (but bratty) ten-year-old twerp. She will be your "tour guide" throughout the book, offering juvenile, snotty, and occasionally helpful random insights on my creative process.

HI! I'm Annoying!

Table of Contents:

Table of discontent

Women's ~~History~~ Hystery

In 1852, a ladies' seminary was established near the San Francisco Bay, in the two-year-old state of California. This school offered girls from nice families a chance to become educated in the more useful arts of womanhood, like music, dancing, poetry, and drama. The best its graduates could look forward to in those days was a career in the domestic sciences; if they were really lucky and smart, they could manage their husband's career. These women could only scheme and dream of voting, earning their own living, or owning their own property.

In 1865 the seminary became Mills, and in 1895, Mills became the first accredited women's college west of the Rockies. At that time women were not admitted into traditional universities or colleges, no matter how gifted or brilliant they were born or raised to be.

Since then, Mills College has always been a protective place for young women to grow their knowledge and develop their talents in a supportive environment away from real-world pressures. After the successful 1990 student strike, every member of the community could recite the reasons why single-sex education was still relevant at the end of a century of integration: Because men in classrooms tend to dominate conversations; because women still make, like, one dollar for every Deutschmark a man makes (and have to make dinner besides); and because sometimes the needs and interests of girls get forgotten or lose their funding when football season comes around or poli-gious conservatives start shouting.

Which is all to say that behind the hysteria of the strike, there was a cherished history worth preserving.

In my first weeks at Mills, I was enchanted by the dark paneled hallways, stucco tiles and musty smells of the old dorms, the quaint collections of old books and rampant teapots. I heard whispered stories about students in Victorian times who used to walk around holding hands (imagine that—affectionate friendships uncolored by sexual labels—woah) and write passionate letters to one another. There used to be a riding stable, and a beauty shop, and rituals where students dressed in gauzy togas and frolicked around Lake Aliso with lanterns in the twilight like Isadora Duncan. Sometimes they even dressed up as George and Martha Washington and danced the gavotte...whatever that is.

The Mills I attended, however, shunned the glee clubs and tea dances, eschewing the coffee, bridge, and cigarette parties of earlier years in favor of athletics. Hooray for aerobics and basketball! The student body was more serious, perhaps more competitive, and more socially guarded. Instead of dancing gavottes with one another they had keggers with Cal frat boys and shook their hair and booties. But there were students from all over the world, and for me, making friends with people from countries and walks of life more "exotic" (a relative term, I know,) than mine was a thrill.

These cartoons are my reflections on the layers of history at Mills.

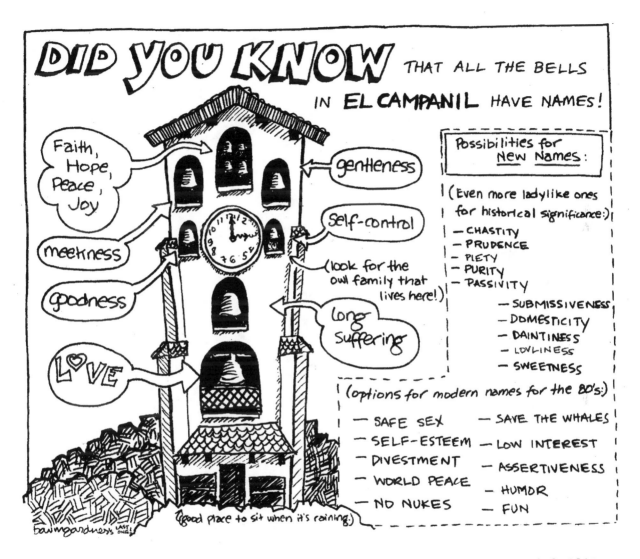

The Campanile, Mills' iconic bell tower built in 1904, is famous for being Julia Morgan's first big commission in 1904. She was America's first woman architect and went on to design numerous gorgeous buildings on the Mills campus and beyond, the biggest and most famous being Hearst Castle. Living at Mills means hearing each of these bells sing every fifteen minutes. All day. Every day. Year in. Year out. And, if you know the meaning of the bells, the virtues they represent are subliminally drilled into your head. Constantly.

A picture hangs in the Alumnae House of past president Aurelia Henry Reinhardt, a mother-of-the-nation type from the 1930s. She looks to the future, and her robes billow out behind her like sails on a schooner. Here in the future, though, we're all a little confused.

A sense of unity tends to prevail when women rally around womanhood, but our differences soon spring open—to catch us in their traps, or to bring us to greater understanding.

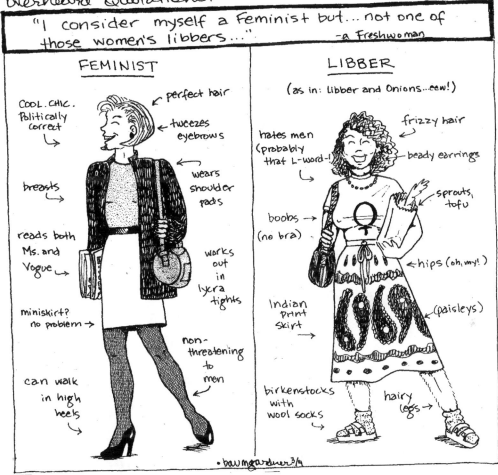

Overheard Quotations:

"I consider myself a Feminist but... not one of those women's libbers..."   —a Freshwoman

FEMINIST

COOL. CHIC. Politically correct

perfect hair

tweezes eyebrows

breasts

wears shoulder pads

reads both Ms. and Vogue

works out in lycra tights

miniskirt? no problem

non-threatening to men

can walk in high heels

LIBBER

(as in: Libber and Onions...eew!)

hates men (probably that L-word-!)

frizzy hair

beady earrings

sprouts, tofu

boobs → (no bra)

hips (oh, my!)

Indian Print Skirt

(paisleys)

birkenstocks with wool socks

hairy legs →

• baumgardner 3/4

For example: every young woman of the eighties had to ask herself: *What kind of woman am I?* A certain character symbolized Mills in the 1980s, to me: the polite, upfront, and assertive Feminist. Unlike the radical expressive feminists you'd find in those days at, say, Sarah Lawrence, the Women's Libbers (as in *Liber*-ationists— there's that freedom thing again) of the 1960s, or the proud, crazy Flappers of the twenties (who brashly wore makeup and smoked cigarettes to claim their own sexual power and pleasure), Upfront Feminists worked the system from within.

Suffragette...Flapper...Libber...Feminist... What's the next highly charged word for "woman who cares"?

— EARLY ATTEMPTS AT SOUP MARKETING

A few years before I got to Mills, the campus beauty shop had closed its doors forever. Why? Did it create an image problem? Did polish become obsolete with the advent of logo sweatpants? I'd like to think it was because the Liberal Arts created so much *inner beauty* in students that hairdos just didn't matter anymore.

The Oakland Living History Project grew out of Fires of Wisdom, the Mills College oral history project. I had the honor of working on this project, and interviewed some fascinating LOLs (Little Old Ladies) who had once been starry-eyed students like myself. Mills women have done some amazing things in the world. Let's keep history alive! Put on a hat and gloves and go to the library. Then have some tea. And after that, go dancing in the moonlight wearing diaphanous robes....

How many of these faces do you recognize?

In "the real world" I'd never realized how many women had made a difference to the real world, and thus to my own life.

At a women's college, these women became front-and-center heroes. She-roes.

Sketching these faces all for a women's history event poster was a lesson I'll never forget.

Even if I forgot some of their names...*

*Do you know who they are? Guess, then see Appendage 1, page 125.

Men of Mills
(and other wildlife)

Life at Mills in the late 1980s was, for me, a smörgåsbord (funny word! Say it out loud—say it with a Swedish accent!) of opportunity. Mills had world-class scholars teaching fine arts, writing, dance, music, and three or four different languages. It had a drama department, sports of all kinds, a literary magazine, and a book arts program. It had a brand-new, state-of-the-art science building (which only lasted twenty years for some strange reason), a computer lab where students could use these amazing new electronic typewriter gizmos called "Apple PCs", and clubs for everything from lesbians to bisexuals. It had everything I'd ever dreamed of, but what did I do? I holed up with my books and drew cartoons.

Starting at Mills halfway through my junior year ("a resumer" in Mills-speak; "a stranger from the outside" in plain English)—my third college well into my twenties—provided me with a determination to focus on my studies. I barely had time to settle in at Mills before I was out of there, and missed all the bonding that happens in one's freshman and sophomore years. But a stranger's perspective is a writer's perspective, so pen in hand, week by week, I just drew what I saw.

Many people who attend women's colleges hear "get thee to a nunnery" jokes on a regular basis. Mills isn't anything like a nunnery, except for the obvious fact that it's lousy with highly devoted females. Ladies, women, girls girls girls, everywhere, all the time. Which, I'm sure, must be a big distraction if you LIKE like girls. But a healthy straight girl such as my-self (by healthy I mean horny) soon found it was just as much a torment NOT to be around boys as it was to be around them. (Exasperated sigh.) It certainly allowed me to focus in a very focused way on the work I was focused on. (Yes! Check out all this sublimated sexual-ity! I was SO prolific at Mills!)

What I'm getting to is this: When men are rare as rooster's lips, you notice them in a different sort of way.

It's embarrassing, for example, to find yourself on the other end of a leering stare, or wolf-whistling in the dark.

But I digress. I was talking about GIRLS here, and being a GIRL, and what GIRLS (like me) do and think about and talk about...wasn't I?

If we could understand flies:

Hystorical footnote! My first scanned & edited cartoons: the curtains were textured with a paint bucket. The ship was my first "cgi" (computer-generated image). Good old MacDraw!

Mills is an idyllic oasis, but being nervous and a little afraid is ever in vogue there. My first work-study job was driving students around the campus at night in the Security Van. Round and round I would go (learning how to go around in circles a little too well, alas). I figured out the lay of the land and got to eavesdrop on—if not meet—all sorts of interesting young women. Coming from a homogeneous midwestern hometown, I was fascinated by the presence of actual Black, Asian, and Jewish people, formerly mythical people of faraway lands and TV. (And until the Nineteen Eighties, not very visible there either.)

Appendage 2 on page 126 has a map of Mills for your convenience.

This cartoon accurately depicts how incredibly dorky I, as a dorky white girl, felt at first around women of color. (A white girl's eternal question: are they cool because they were black or are they just cool?) Secretly, I was relieved that no one seemed to be bothered by this cartoon. Secretly I longed to have such frank, fascinating, and linguistically provocative conversations about race in real life, not just in my imagination. Secretly I longed to have actual friends, as well.

I was never sure which thoughts I should share, and which I should keep to myself. Cartooning was always an experiment. I was learning a lot about the world... but the world was also changing rapidly around me.

In the late 1980s, several curious things were happening in the world other than AIDS, Greenpeace and Self-Esteem. For example, Nancy Reagan tried to stop addictive drug use with her "Just Say No" campaign, and her husband Ronnie tried to stop the Cold War with his Strategic Defense Initiative, also known as "Star Wars." But far more powerful than the Reagans were two kinds of PCs: Personal Computers and Political Correctness.

Political Correctness burned like a wildfire through the lazy language habits of mainstream America, rooting out power struggles in everyday speech.

I couldn't quite manage to get the potential funniness that the concept of "Safe Love" promised into a cartoon. Thankfully, a friend pointed out it should probably be a country-western song instead (see Appendage 3).

"Es wirkt!"

"Free" speech was challenged to grow up and become "Less Harmful" speech. "Isms" of all kinds (racism, sexism, elitism) lurked in the most innocent of sentences. "It's just a joke" was no longer an excuse.

When someone would say, "That's not PC," it was like a linguistic citizen's arrest that could send the speaker into a spiral of embarrassment and self-analysis, if not straight-out social shame.

I discussed this phenomenon (and many others) at length with my very funny advisor, who happened to be like, nine feet tall (and had, therefore, a unique perspective on all humanity). He encouraged me to see things on both concrete and abstract levels, and explore my academic questions creatively. His partner in the German department stood about four feet tall—in stilettos.

This cartoon illustrated a field trip to an exhibit on German Expressionism. ("Es wirkt" means "it worked.")

With a German class three mornings a week for eighteen months (I registered on impulse and got hooked), I spent a lot of time in the Lucie Stern language building (next page), where languages were spoken. Twenty years later, I hear "The Plant" still does their morning leaf-blowing right when classes begin. Twenty years later, students still wonder: "Are those guys high?" But back then, this was the first of my cartoons that ruffled feathers on campus.

When I drew a marijuana leaf on the back of a "Plant" worker's jacket, I unintentionally activated the stereotype that Mexicans are all stoners. (Searching my soul, I now realize I had that celebrity advocate of Latino Artists, that pioneer of broadcast Hispanic advancement, comedian Cheech Marin to thank for subliminally imprinting this stereotype on my tender sixth grade psyche.) This was part of my lesson that *all* comic arts rely on stereotyping, artful or not. And in my heart, kindness and comedy kind of compete.

See Appendage 4 for angry rants. 17

But those Plant Guys deserved better than that! They were, being Male Humans, a rare and special species at Mills. A few years before I'd arrived at Mills, the "Men of Arizona State" calendar had made pop-culture history. The idea of doing one for Mills was as un-PC as could be, but completely irresistible since rumors were already circulating about Mills going coed.

Reactions were strong—though sharply divided between uproariously amused and incredibly offended. (A few of my subjects were mildly flattered, like the grad students in Halloween costume

18

MEN OF MILLS COLLEGE *pin-up calendar*

JANUARY FEBRUARY MARCH APRIL

MAY JUNE JULY AUGUST

SEPTEMBER OCTOBER NOVEMBER DECEMBER

@baumgardner'00

(LET'S KEEP IT THIS WAY!)

and the unicycle-riding ultra-nerd who ended up as my roommate in the campus apartments senior year.) But even though I had reason to think the lithe and groovy crew team would find their role representing Mills' mythical cranky bull-dykes amusing, I completely misjudged that one and (ouch) hurt some feelings.

I took my discipline—a few weeks off the paper—and later tried to make it up to everyone with a Politically Correct version of my idea. This one made everyone laugh. Except math majors...they saw calculators instead of calendars.

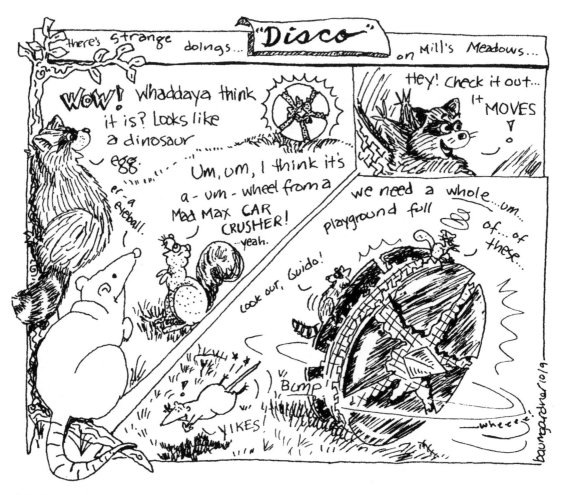

I had enough on my plate to deal with, without stirring up pointless controversy. It's so much easier to avoid anything remotely political. At one time I wanted to start a series* about cute talking campus wildlife. (This one celebrates the installation of a very cool sculpture by Arnaldo Pomodoro on the Toyon Meadow.)

Honestly, Mills is a beautiful place. It's a green oasis in the heart of an asphalt city. It's a sanctuary for all kinds of nature—not just maidenfolk obsessed with non-existent men.

*First in a series of one!

Right across the road from my dorm room was a man-made pond we called "the frog pond," where the croakers sang love songs to the rain. But up the road, the real concerts were held at the stream-fed, cattail-clogged Lake Aliso, where the bassos, tenors and chirpers thundered so loud after the rain that they drowned out the noise from the highway. Those frogs (and my science professor) made an environmentalist out of me.

But apparently even cute talking animals think about sex.

And apparently even innocent furry animals could be connected, in my busy little mind, with masculine swarthiness.

So what's a lonely girl to do?

On my own in vast California, in a place like Mills to focus, I was seeking something that could only come from within.

Something feminine.

Something about wisdom...power...balance...confidence...cuteness.... All rolled together in one.

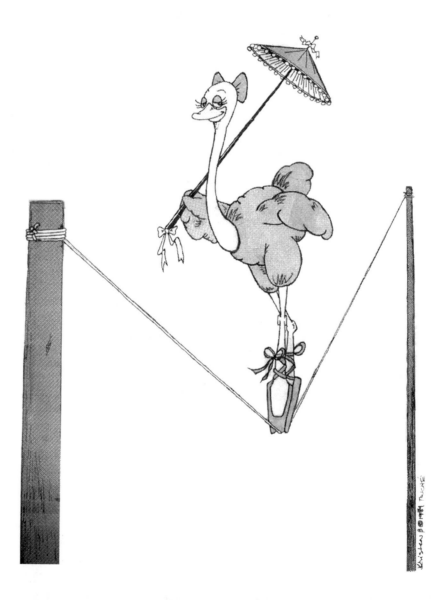

3

str_^Estrogen

The greatest benefit to life on a single-sex campus is that you know why you're there: to get an education. You can really focus on your work. Which is good, because there's a lot of it. Mills students are hard workers. They read. They study. They write. They dance. They research. They do internships. They do work-study jobs. They take tests. They read some more.

Sometimes they take a break. But then they go back to work. And realize their break was too long. So they have to work harder. And somewhere in there they might find a moment to TOTALLY STRESS OUT. About how their roommate/boyfriend/girlfriend is being a jerk. Or about how they are going to pay for the next round of tuition. Or how they are ever going to figure out this brain-wrenching math problem. Or about how they are going to fit in all the cool classes they want to take before they graduate. Or about HOW MUCH WORK THEY HAVE TO DO.

With all the work I had to do, sometimes I barely had time to cartoon. Often I'd finish my drawings at the last minute, handing them in with the ink barely dry, with no time to re-do my lettering and make the 'e's any more legible.

One of my many make-ends-meet jobs was illustrating for my mom, who followed me out to California to pursue her own career as a writer and public speaker. As a community psychologist and parent educator, one of the topics she was an expert on was, yes, STRESS!

By always keeping the rights to my drawings, I was able to use them for *The Weekly* when I couldn't make a deadline. Conversely, whenever I had some great inspiration that wouldn't work for her materials, I could still use it in my strip. As a budding environmentalist, I was always excited to find new ways to recycle.

The cartoons in this chapter all illustrate the various ways Mills students find, eternally, to cope (or not cope) with stress.

Eating...

Exercise...

...after a week of rest and atrophy, Jane's gran plié gets the better of her.

This cartoon explains why I was no good at ballet. I got this image in my head the first day after spring break and giggled so much I couldn't keep my mind on my feet.

Avoidance...

~ CRAMMING ON MILLS BEACH ~

baumgardner - 4/87

Mills Beach was, alternatively: poolside near the Tea Shop (where the plaza is now); in the middle of Orchard Meadow; on a crowded hill-dorm balcony; or in the Greek Theater. Almost always a guerilla effort, pursued only by the brave.

Denial...

**Problems? Me?
Of course not!**

One of my early illustrations for my mom. You may notice in the signatures of these cartoons how I flirted, for years, with a variety of pen names. "Kristen Baumgardner" always seemed way too long and clumsy and un-glamorous. Just one of those many little things that stressed me out.

The dangers of denial. We all know ostriches don't really stick their heads in the sand. But what if they did? And what if they couldn't read?

Getting Help...

Advice Columnist's Nightmare

baumgardner
10/16/87

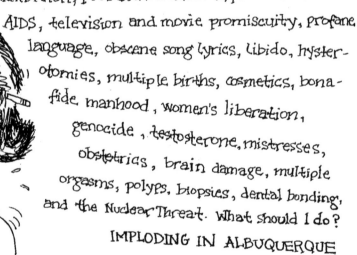

" Dear Ann Slanders,

I'm concerned about tight blue jeans, public nudity, teen pregnancy, anorexia nervosa, bust reductions, bust enhancements, tush tucks, tummy tucks, thigh-firming exercises, contraception, exhibition, prosthetic devices, prostitutes, AIDS, television and movie promiscuity, profane language, obscene song lyrics, libido, hysterotomies, multiple births, cosmetics, bona-fide manhood, women's liberation, genocide, testosterone, mistresses, obstetrics, brain damage, multiple orgasms, polyps, biopsies, dental bonding, and the Nuclear Threat. What should I do?

IMPLODING IN ALBUQUERQUE

 Hysterotomies? Is that when you have your hysteria removed?

Q. Why didn't the Ancient Greeks have Psychoanalysis?

I wrote a five-page paper on this topic before realizing it was better expressed as a cartoon.

Complaining...

Talk about stressful. This political cartoon utilized cute animals to express my concern that Robert Bork, Reagan's pro-life Supreme Court candidate, would ultimately overturn the reproductive (or non-reproductive) rights that women had fought for centuries to define.

All of the above...

and...

Surrender.

© K.Caven

This was the first illustration I ever did for money, advertising a yoga class. I give copies of it to my dentists, electrologists, and GYNs, so strangers have to stare at it when they are in awkward positions.

4

prehistoric
easter
bunny

My Brain
on Holiday

A good theme can turn a creative block into a block party. Six or eight times a year, I got to come up with a cartoon on a holiday theme. I loved the freedom allowed by my editor at *The Weekly* and the Mills Community (even the freedom to make mistakes). I could be as cute and weird as I wanted with nobody around to say "I don't get it" or "that's not funny, try this instead." Or, "get back to your studies/your homework/your chores/the real world." And no one ever said, "don't quit your day job." (Since none of us had one.)

A blank page was playtime. I could sit down and try to translate a silly idea that had distracted me in class, make a Jesus joke, or create a world where bunnies and dinosaurs were scientifically comparable. I could make wearing garlic a public health issue, and create characters out of anything I wanted. Even eggs. And sperms.

The fact is, I had come to Mills with a sperm in my back pocket. Eew, sorry, that sounds gross—what I mean is a paper doll of a sperm with little manly costumes to wear. I had drawn Sammy Sperm my freshman year when we played God in science, making chicken zygotes come to life under a microscope.

The magnetic Emily Egg was born at Mills, naturally...where I no longer drew *generic 'he'* characters. She is Sammy Sperm's guiding force; she is his grail, his goal, his reason for being. Sammy and Emily were life-creating gods, costumed supergametes, spirit guides who brought me, many times, to the deeper questions of life like, *Where do we come from?* And, *Why are high heels so important?* They played the romantic leads every Valentine's Day—known on college campuses everywhere as the feast-day of National Condom Week.

The first holiday of every school year, however, is always Halloween.

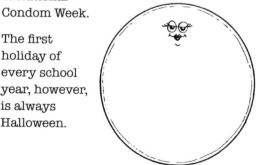

FRESHMAN PLAYING GOD:

zap!

EGGIES

Spermies

Halloween

Thanksgiving Break

See Appendages for a bonus Thanksgiving cartoon!

Christmas Break

"WELL, FRANKINCENSE IS HARD TO COME BY THESE DAYS."

Must have been a busy week... this was recycled from my high school paper in the early '80s. But I love recycling!

Valentine's Day 1987

National Condom Week Theatre presents:

THE ADVENTURES OF: Sammy Sperm *!

* a.k.a Speramus

ALAS, MY BELOVED EGGBE... I FEAR I FIND NO CHINK IN THIS STRANGE WALL OF PLASTICK THROUGH WHICH OUR HANDS MIGHT INTERTWINGLE....

K. Baumgardner 2/16/87

Emily Egg's first appearance (a problem of scale). Get it? Pyramus and Thisbe?

Valentine's Day 1988

What a difference a year made! And that difference was: MacPaint!

Ash Wednesday

And....

A SCIENTIFIC COMPARISON OF the KANGAROO and TYRANNOSAURUS REX:

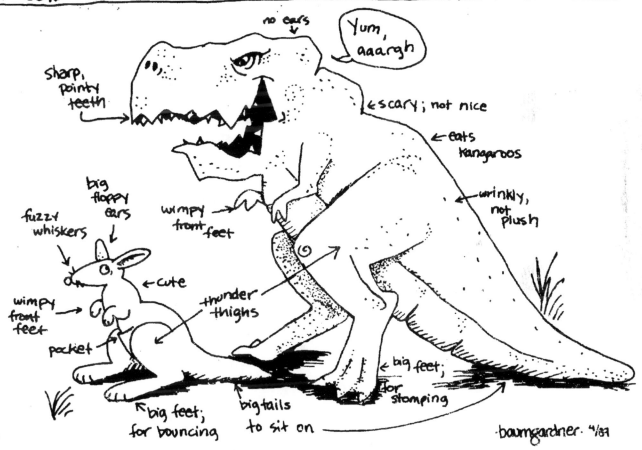

Easter Break!

COMPARISON OF KANGAROO AND EASTER BUNNY

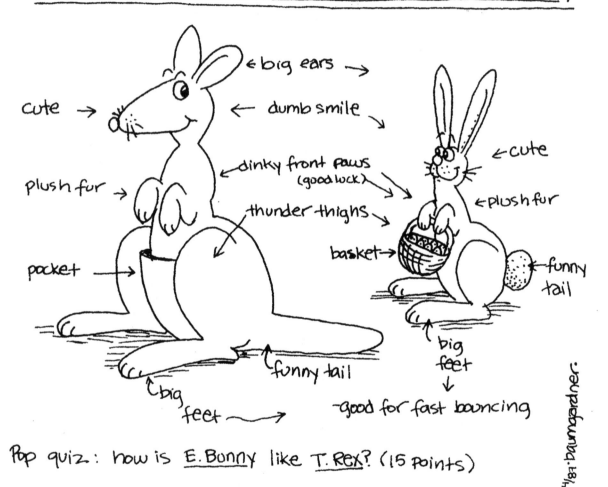

cute →

← big ears →

← dumb smile

dinky front paws (good luck)

plush fur →

thunder thighs

pocket →

funny tail

big feet →

←cute

←plush fur

basket →

←funny tail

big feet ↓

good for fast bouncing

4/87 baumgardner.

Pop quiz: how is E. Bunny like T. Rex? (15 points)

Get it? Feel like you've been on a mental vacation?

5

Graphic Novelties

Cartooning is an amazing medium. Like fine art, it comes from a single creative mind that has somehow, miraculously, found in this world permission to express itself. Like film, it relies on both words and images to convey more subtle shades of meaning. But unlike film—which relies on chemicals, casting, collaboration and loads of cash—in cartooning, one person can be enough. The tools are low tech; a big investment in materials set me back less than a hundred bucks.* With only a comfortable place to work and a little (well, a lot of) time, an artist can create a world. And with the unlimited potential of a blank page, the practical applications for cartooning as a communications tool are an open horizon. When I discovered Larry Gonnick's *A Cartoon History of the Universe*, I found support for my theory that cartoons could be used to explore complex ideas. When I discovered Art Spiegelman's Pulitzer Prize-winning graphic novel *Maus*, I found hope for my literary aspirations. In my ideal future, there would be as many genres of cartoon literature as there were text-only books.

Between drawing cartoons for *The Weekly*, I managed to find more ways to draw more cartoons. Here I was with this obscure, whimsical craft, literally at my fingertips, and a head full of serious questions, like: *How does language work?* We communicate in so many different ways and on so many different levels that we cannot even be aware of every message we send. *Why are some things meaningful to some people and completely insignificant to others?* And with such a vast code of information flowing through every mind, every second of every day, *can anyone ever actually fully understand anyone else?* Our cultural assumptions are complex mythologies— evolved over centuries, or sometimes just years— that have so much power over our actions and can create such soaring good or plunging evil; *how can we be aware of, or influence these mythologies?*

So you see, it was not all about talking sperms.

Between 1984 and 1994 I created about fifty pages of comix (note: spelling comics with an 'x' conveys edginess and artsiness) on topics ranging from science to soul-searching. In this chapter I present stories about and samples of these daring departures from my hungry typewriter.

*Pencils, a gum eraser, a Rapidograph pen, paper, a metal ruler, an exacto knife, rubber cement, and several sheets of transparent adhesive patterns to use as background texture, if you must know.

KiDo Comic

I always noticed that in order to learn something I would have to get a good picture of it in my head, and I wondered if sharing these pictures was a way I could help other people learn.

Back at my first college, my Tae Kwon Do teacher was intrigued with the idea, and we attempted a collaboration on his training manual.

As great an idea as it was, this project was cut short by the insurmountable obstacles of no one having any money and me leaving to go to art school.

Does it hurt your eyes to try to read this? Sorry! Read the last paragraph on page 55 real quick...

Atomic Comic

After Sammy Sperm was "released" from my imagination, my science teacher encouraged me to harness my powers for good (rather than distracting my classmates). So, rather than regurgitate a semester's lessons on the history of science term paper, I decided to try a cartoon narrative.

Cartooning is as time consuming as it is fun; I was only able to complete three pages, turning chapters two through four in as prose. My professor was impressed, and helped me apply for a grant to finish the project over summer vacation.

I knocked myself out on the application, elated at the thought of such meaningful work, hoping to immerse myself in cartoon science.

But I didn't get the support. They disqualified my project because the rules specifically stated the grant was for *writing* a science project, not *drawing* one.

Falling between such cracks became the dark side of my cartooning ambition.

Publishers tend to want to publish stuff that they're already publishing, and I had a hard time finding anyone who was already publishing what I wanted to publish.

Had I found an art school that offered classes in Graphic Novels or ways to combine Art and Science at the time,

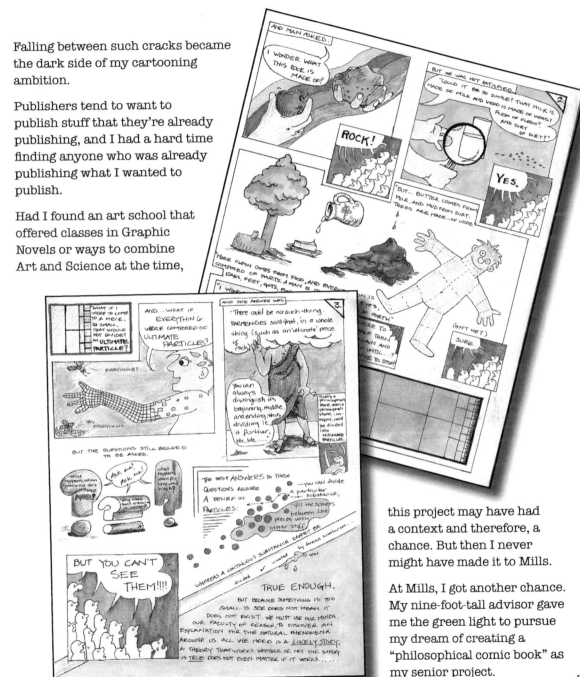

this project may have had a context and therefore, a chance. But then I never might have made it to Mills.

At Mills, I got another chance. My nine-foot-tall advisor gave me the green light to pursue my dream of creating a "philosophical comic book" as my senior project.

51

My Mistress Opus

Knowing little to nothing, really, about the art form of comics (save a childhood filled with *Archie* and *Mad Magazine*), I leapt off the cliff and learned to fly on the way down.

The Reason She Left is about a young woman on a quest for knowledge. Sound familiar? She looks a little like me, and her name is Nettie (short for Netsirk, probably, which is *Kristen* spelled backwards). But Nettie is not me, nor is her story the same as mine.

I created Nettie as a personification of the feminine intellect, a spirit that craves genuine connection of ideas and ideals. She helped me to examine the central philosophical question that brought me to Mills: *are women's experiences relevant to society's highest cultural ideals?*

Her own questions push her out of the safe, known world she has outgrown (called, in this story, "The Citadel of Reason"). She enters a wider world to seek her own truth, to figure out who she is, to find answers. She finds friends.

Nettie's journey took her through 31 pages of Deep Thoughts, including to some sticky stuff about logic vs. intuition, objectivity vs. subjectivity, and the slippery delights and terrors of existential post-modernism.

...after a few pages of childhood games gave her the distinct impression the universe was a dualistic and competitive place, we find Nettie in college.

In the end, Nettie meets someone who shares her questions, which helps her understand herself and find the balance she seeks.

Had enough? Want more?

Look for *The Reason She Left and Other Stories*, which contains complete versions of all of the "graphic novelties" in this chapter —and more!

55

Princess Comic

This action-packed Cinderella story was literally a dream that came alive through my ink pen. I had this dream after I'd graduated from Mills, just before I began my own romantic odyssey towards marriage and family.

In the last twenty years, the world has refreshed itself with assertive heroines, many of them ass-kicking warrior-princesses. But that morning I woke up shocked and amazed at this gift from my subconsious.

The dream was prescient of so many real things in my life: a reckoning with my father (a doctor) and my stepfamily; finding a group of fun and gentle girlfriends who would see me through; and even a magical white gown that led to some remarkable feminine adventures and literary larks.

Later, I began writing an opera about friendships between non-fairy princesses, which evolved into my musical, *Shoes, a Mirror, and a Big, Pink Rose,* which is on a meandering adventure to the big stage.

6

The World Outside

My proudest moment at Mills was on graduation day, when I stood back and watched my friends and family giggle and exclaim at all of the cartoons you have just read. Along with a few of my paintings, they were all mounted on striking black backgrounds and hung on the clean white walls of a small, sunny gallery in Mills' brand new Art Center. I flitted about in a giddy, altered state: *If I am having a real art show in a fine art gallery, am I living up to my childhood dream?*

As witnessed by my childhood fascination with zipper pulls and my satirical self-portrait as a "glamorous cartoonist" (frontispiece), I always associated "arrival" at one's destination symbolizing success with some sort of "glamourosity." Eventually, I would find that life is full of such "arrivals," each of them marking a departure, as well, into a whole new set of unknowns. My "arrival" in the gallery slipped quickly into the past, and soon I moved on from Mills.

My portfolio of cartoons and my graphic novel-ish philosophical comic book later became my entry tickets to the (glamorous) secret clubs where all the (glamorous) cartoonists hung out.

But on that day in the gallery, a sweet friend gave me a graduation card that showed a gal in a cap and gown flying through the air. The caption read, *A strong wind took Mary on a career path she'd never intended.* This image crystallized my hope of being swept up by something interesting. What might I become? A graphic novelist? A designer of greeting cards such as that one? A stripper—of the cartoon variety or otherwise? I hoped that, no matter what I did, I'd be on a path that included ART. After all, I had an image of myself at thirty to try to live up to....

But first I had to find a place where that wind could catch me. I traveled for a while, working at a summer camp and expanding my collection of international friends to share the road. But life kept calling me back to Oakland. After all, all my stuff was there.

A Sense of Place

Only in Marin

Stouffer's

lobster
shortcake

This drawing was recycled from an art-school exercise. My weekly editor captioned it for california.

Oakland.
Land of Oaks.
The East Bay.
City Across the Bay.

Murder Capital of the World....

As a young lass, safe in the gated queendom that was Mills, I had imagined a world of threatening thugs and gangsters lurking outside. There they waited to rob me, ravage me, or worse: speak to me in a version of English I couldn't understand.

ax me what's wrong wid dis queschin

Gosh, even my imaginary bad guys were adorable!

Once I began to venture out, however, I got to know my new home and learned to love it. I lived in (glamorous) San Francisco for a while, but Oakland's sunny Lake Merritt brought me back. I would get some of my dumbest ideas there.

There was much to discover in this wide world, in the cosmopolitan, metropolitan, neapolitan Bay Area....

First in a series of one —new myths and legends of the Bay Area. The next in the series was supposed to be about the Van Ness Monster. I could never find the time, so I gave the idea to a friend. (See Appendage 6)

Mr. MacArthur

by billie boomerang

A local paper started up, and the editor invited me to do a cartoon strip. What a breeze! I knew something about that! I did one cartoon for the *MacArthur Metro* before leaving town to travel and live all over God-knows where. Now it's my neighborhood news.

But who the heck is Billie Boomerang?

I love naming things, and I've always been pretty good at it. I've left my mark on many businesses, books, clubs, and dogs. But I always felt my own name was too much of a mouthful. In second grade I was always the last to turn in my papers because it took so long to write "Baumgardner" at the top of the page. (I vowed to marry a man with a short last name.)

So as long as I was having fun cartooning, why not use a kicky nom-de-plume?

I tried "*Aster Gardner" (with an asterisk, how cute is that), "Lola Posole," "Billie Boomerang," simply "Baumgardner," and even "*SCRIBBLE*," but nothing ever stuck. Meanwhile I always seemed to default to "Kristen Baumetc."

First in a series of one. Alas, consistency was not a muse of mine.

Not the Only One

Life, if you do all your work, is a see-saw in this way: you start school as a kindergarten baby and soon you're a gigantic and smart fifth grader, only to become a puny sixth grader when you get to middle school. At the top of the heap as an eighth grader, you then start high school as a nobody. As a big-cheese high school senior, you're on top of the world, then you start college, out of context, confused, lowly, but with anything possible. A few years later, you're Big (Wo)Man on Campus again, and go out on top. Ta-da. Then bam, you're suddenly starting over again: a freshman in the school of life.

After I graduated, I missed my friends, my scholarly routines, my job at *The Weekly*, and my friends from all the schools I'd ever attended. They all went on to new places and I wasn't sure what was next, where I fit in, or even, again, what my "major" in Life would be.

On a quest to find somewhere I could belong, I went in search of other cartoonists. I took classes, attended lectures, joined clubs, and I met some. I went to parties. I met some famous strippers. I met some of my cartoon idols. I even discovered a world of cartoonists, just like me. I loved hanging out with men again. Adorable, funny guys. We watched a lot of Star Trek and ate popcorn.

But I wanted more!

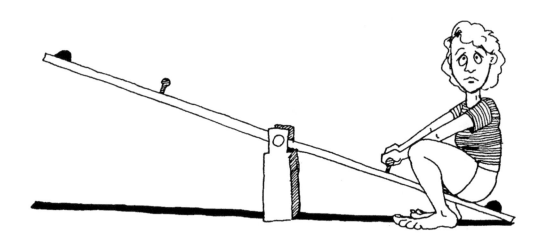

High Society

I was young! I wanted to dance! I had come all this way, and now I wanted a circle of Beautiful People to hobnob with! I wanted to rub elbows with intellectuals and international playboys! I wanted caviar, music, and champagne! I wanted my hand to be kissed, all the way up my arm, like in the Addams family.

I wanted GLAMOUR, darnit! Hadn't I made that clear?

And somehow, finally, I found it.

As someone interested in images and the stories they tell; as someone living in a constant state of identity crisis; as someone who didn't own a skirt... I wanted to learn more about the self-defining power of lipstick.

My timing was good. Retro was IN!

I found the people who could teach me. They were bohemians, revolutionaries in the glamour underground who lived to bring another era back to life. Living out of time, each of them was gifted with outrageous multiple talents and movie-star charm that oozed from their miniscule pores. They wore vintage clothes and threw fabulous parties in historic buildings. They could quote old movies and burst into songs that hadn't been heard on the radio for fifty years.

Do not cross the lipstick lines.

Can't you see, I'll bleed?

I had studied The Classics; but the classics to these cool cats meant black and white movies with touch-dancing and cigarettes. I had learned classical music; they showed me jazz. I had studied ancient history; now I was ready to wallow in my own century—up to my knees, up to my neck, up to the mole I drew on my cheek.

The behatted women and bespatted men I met in San Francisco's Art Deco Society, ten years before the millennium, challenged me to bring my energy out into real time in a way I hadn't done since lip-synching to Louis Armstrong in a big white dress my first month at Mills.

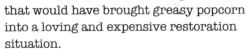

I soon found a shade of red lipstick that worked for me. I soon found myself in front of flashing cameras. I soon found myself on stage wearing a vintage bathing suit and carrying a beach ball—much to the horror of my inner libber. (My inner feminist liked making a statement.)

Baring my thighs in public—on TV no less, and generally drawing attention to myself, I was able to both discover my inner extrovert and connect myself with history in a very real way. One of my first acts was to help save the imagination-saturated Paramount Theater in Oakland from an expansion that would have brought greasy popcorn into a loving and expensive restoration situation.

Hamming it up at modeling and dancing, I rarely found a solitary moment to draw. And when I did, I realized what I missed out on alone with my paper with pen: the sound of applause.

Cartooning is a solitary art. You don't get to see your fans. You don't hear their laughter. You also don't, routinely, get to spark off the energy of others who are brighter, smarter, or better dressed. It's all you.

My adventures as a bathing beauty/femme fatale took me to places I'd never dreamed, like the wind that blew the cartoon graduate on that greeting card.

I adored the old cartoons and artwork from the early days of 20th century advertising and pop culture, and discovered the magic of clip art for my graphic design. My own drawings could never be as complete, as deft, as—you know—*classic*. My sketchbook from that time contains very little. This comic panel, referencing 1950's Best Picture, *All About Eve*, seemed a little too... um, *unsophisticated* to submit to the society papers.

  First in a series of one.... About celebrity poo-poo jokes.

In Love with an Idea

Steeped in the stylized romance of old Hollywood, my thoughts eventually turned to love. As a "slave to my creative urges," I wondered if I would ever be able to go where love led. As a fundamentally silly person, I wondered if I would ever be able to get serious about partnership. Would I ever be able to lead anything resembling a normal life?

MATINEE

by billie boomerang © 1989

There was no standing ovation. He knew it was our own fault; this bumpkin afternoon audience had clapped between all the movements.

But he was a gentleman and didn't reprimand us. He just bowed politely and gave us a brilliant encore -- that went over most of our heads.

My date kept staring at me meaningfully. He had breath like a horse.

The second encore drew a *walking* ovation by much of the audience. They headed out into a world with a backbeat. But then, a voice in the back cried out,

Polonaise! Polonaise!

I don't know if he took the suggestion, or even heard it, but he played the third encore with a certain gusto. **Lovely.** I wished it would *never* end............

One of my favorite cartoons was by another Mills alumna, Gail Machlis. A mother shouts to a father while holding a phone to her ear: "She's called to say she's fallen in love...with an idea."

That was totally me. I used my dates as an excuse to enjoy cultural experiences. I could spend the whole time lost in thought, trolling for funny stories I could write about when I got home.

when writers meet

One cool guy I hung out with said, "I could never marry another writer." At that moment I realized two things: 1) I was a writer, and 2) I wanted to marry a writer.

But finding the right writer was beyond me. The ones I dated creeped me out. And the whole marriage thing freaked me out. I didn't want to get married just for the sake of getting married.

I did get close a couple times. I even found myself holding hands with a special boy outside city hall one crisp spring morning.

Actually, we were both, at the time, also holding hands with strangers, and it wasn't really city hall, it was San Francisco's Federal building. And we weren't trying go get in; we were trying to keep workers out, in protest of the Gulf War.

It was so romantic. We got to hang out in handcuffs together for the rest of the day.

But back in second grade, war had disturbed me deeply. I had protested Vietnam wearing a sandwich board that read "War is a No-No," and I'd vowed back then to fight war all my life. Just think of the devastating prices women and children have to pay over years, decades, and centuries for the hot-headed politics of men....

Saving the World

Dog of War
eats a
Peace Chick

Sitting next to my cute, pony-tailed boy all day with my usually-busy hands tied up in a plastic twist-tie, I thought about how I might use my cartoons to get people thinking about how the choices they make MATTER.

Planet of Slow Learners was a series of three cartoons inspired by a poster I saw at one protest. Mills had made me an environmentalist, and information was scattered everywhere. I found a creative way to channel my anxiety: organizing all the facts into one place.

I easily published these three panels in a free local start-up paper, with plans for future episodes on cars, food, and alternate energy sources. But *The Paper* folded (an unfortunate pun) and I lost my momentum.

Digging these panels out of my files after so many years, however, I feel a sense of relief that they no longer appear to be as revolutionary as they seemed when I drew them. Less than twenty years later, Earth Day really is becoming a holiday for the Earth. And golly, she really needs it.

Not many people saw *Planet of Slow Learners*, so the cartoons never really lived up to their potential to make the cultural difference I wished they could. But I'd like to think the letters I wrote, the guerilla flyers I designed, the recycling programs I started, the conversations I held, and the dollars I donated made a difference. Today, maybe because we've gone too far, people—and governments even—are starting to get it.

See Appendages 7 & 8 for some activist graphics.

My No-Date Mate

For someone like me who had had troubles with men, and who had found her center in their absence, I was lucky to find one who could navigate all my multiple mixed messages. And still like me.

Yes, in one of life's most astonishing twists, I found myself suddenly engaged to the funniest loud-and-obnoxious smart-ass I knew from high school.

He's the guy who named a talking sperm Sammy. He's the guy who teased me about getting to a nunnery. He's the guy who suggested the "safe love" cartoon should be a country-western song.

And yes, he's a writer.

Once he even wrote the curriculum for a very bad college class...that might have been taught at Mills in the 1950s.

> **How to Fake an Orgasm 101:**
> Step One: "Ooh baby, ooh baby, ooh baby."
> Step Two: "Give it to me, lover man."
> Step Three: "God, you're good."
> Step Four: repeat step one.

And on top of it all, he had a nice, short last name.

Ooh, baby.

ooh baby, ooh, baby, ooh baby...

7

Doodling
for Dollars

Does the world really need more art? I used to wonder this while passing craft fairs full of art prints of watercolor boats, while snooping around in used book stores. If the world stopped right now, and no one ever wrote another sentence or drew another line, there would still be so much to read, view, and contemplate, that it would take a million lifetimes to enjoy it all. But there are reasons, compelling reasons, for humans to keep producing art, which includes music and literature, of course. First and foremost, because that's what humans do. Art is an expression of the times and cultures in which we live, evidence of our presence in the material world. Secondly, it just plain FEELS GOOD to make art, and feeling good is a key to happiness, the ultimate motivator.

And thirdly, because sometimes one needs a sandwich.

The reality of the "real" world hit me. My rent and groceries were no longer handled through scholarships and financial aid packages. I wanted to go study art somewhere, but my student loans were enormous. Since I had no money, I made time in my life to learn and create art. I spent a few solid hours each day writing, painting, sketching and inking, or just wandering around and getting inspired. My commitment to art prevented me from pursuing a proper career, much less a nine-to-five job, but I soon realized I had to find some way to support my art habit.

There are five or six ways to have art in your life when you're living in the real world.

    1) drawing for free

    2) drawing on the job

    3) drawing *as* a job

    4) drawing off the clock

    5) getting successfully published

    6) becoming independently wealthy.

I tried them all.

Drawing for a Cause (drawing for free)

...comes in many shades other than beige...

Mere moments after I graduated, a Mills alumna approached me for help with fundraising for the non-profit where she worked. I couldn't have been more flattered, since the previous year's fundraising letter had been written by the illustrious Nicole Hollander, creator of cartoon columnist *Sylvia*. Big shoes to fill. Big, designer shoes, with a matching handbag. I tried not to intimidate myself.

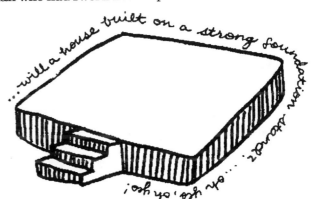

...providing support for women of all shapes and sizes...

Taking a breezy tone, I put on my philosophizing hat and turned "The Women's Foundation" over to my muses. Three things came to mind:

- foundation garments
- foundation makeup, and
- real estate.

I wrote about how women are the foundation of families, civilizations, and all the good things in life. I waxed romantic, yes indeed I did.

Afterwards, my contact at The Women's Foundation forwarded a disgruntled letter from a woman who had sworn not to open her checkbook again...but my letter convinced her otherwise. Success! (Of an odd sort.)

The fundraising letter I wrote kicked off a long and fulfilling career in volunteering. An essential part of being a liberal (as in: *free*) artist.

...will a house built on a strong foundation stand up? oh yes, oh yes!

Doodle Time (drawing on the job)

I had never been to camp as a child, and felt I'd missed some classic life experience. So right out of college, I went to summer camp, getting a staff job in Southern California. I found plenty of ways to be artsy on the job—designing maps, t-shirts, and once, with a friend, even sculpting a 5-foot Raschenberg-inspired paper clip out of an old piece of plumbing pipe. (It's still in my garage, keeping my tarpaulins organized.)

This was in the post-hippie, let's-get-this-grooviness-organized era that brought us "New Games." A slip of the tongue turned "New Lawn Games" into "Nude Lawn Games." It wasn't very long until "Naked Lawn Games" became the staff's inside joke.

☜ This was the official t-shirt design.

☟ This was the unofficial t-shirt design.

82

When summer was over, I started looking for a "real" job. What a nerve-wracking experience! I didn't know what I wanted to do. How could I fit myself into the mold of what people were looking for? One useless tip I got from a friend for combating anxiety was to imagine my potential new boss in his underwear.

Unfortunately, this vivid image, which I managed to carve into my imagination with my pencil, prohibited me from ever wanting to interview anywhere, ever. Just in case I met a guy who looked anything like this.

I finally went to a temp agency, where I could take a test and they could match me up with someone who needed some help.

A year later when I visited Mills, I caught up with my old nine-foot-tall advisor and told him I had been temping.

"Kelly Girl?" He laughed.

"No," I frowned. "MANPOWER."

BIG fan of sock garters, by the way.

Pen for Hire (drawing as a job)

Filing mountains of paperwork for a basement full of brilliant but disgruntled nuclear physicists gave me lots of time to write and draw on the job. One of them later turned to high-tech consulting and hired me to cartoon an ad campaign based on "better mousetraps."

He described to me what the cartoon should look like. I drew it. He hated it. I went back to the drawing board over and over again. AARGH! It was a unique torture drawing to his exacting specifications, but... it paid for a sandwich or two.

Bill — (In Voice)

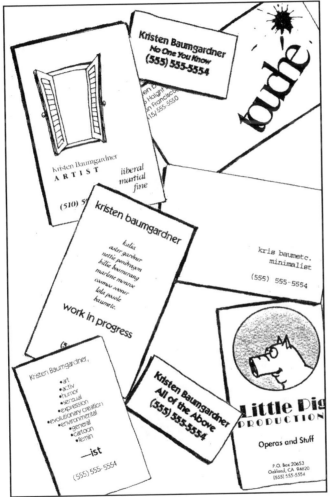

The next thing I drew up was a template for an invoice, so I could look a little more professional when charging clients to draw for them.

I printed up business cards and hung out my proverbial shingle. (I've hung so many shingles I could be a roofer.)

No one ever called... maybe it was the fake Hollywood number... ha ha.

"The Fight Guy"
by Kristen Caven

Touché was my first officially licensed business; the name inspired by a few seasons dabbling in the noble art of fencing. One of my favorite jobs was for a fight choreographer who asked only that I draw him "bristling with weapons" for his company logo. When he went to Afghanistan, they gave him a really big gun. But he tries not to use it.

Vous avez de la bière allemande?
Un express, s'il vous plaît.

Voilà. Une bière et un express.

An interesting, "cutting edge" job came from a Mills student whose senior project combined her double major of French and Computer Science. She was creating a computer program that taught French.

A revolutionary idea at the time.

After seeing these stunning computer animations of mine, an anonymous Mills alumna invited me to a secret lab that was being secretly called the "Lucas/Apple Umbrella," or "LUAU" for short. I swore myself to secrecy when I went to visit... but now I'm going to spill the beans and tell you about the amazing new thing I saw: It's called "interactive video."

There was a projected image of a map that allowed you to *zoom in,* going into deeper detail the closer you got to street level. My guide told me there were plans to map out the entire *country!* And put it up so the public could see it, when they hooked up their PCs to this new thing called *"The World Wide Web."*

There, I've told someone. Hard to keep that a secret for twenty years. It blew my mind!

But what I was looking at was the rest of my life. We'd all be swimming in technology within a decade, and my life would be inextricably intertwingled with the evolution of the Apple PC.

But further attempts to find work where science and art combined did not manifest. Instead, I tended to attract clients who were healers, learning some valuable lessons about business along the way.

Sometimes I would have a wonderful, professional relationship with a client, like the nun-mentor who wrote booklets that helped brand-new nuns find their way. She'd ask for what she wanted, I'd draw it, I'd send her an invoice, and she'd pay it.

And sometimes things would get a little muddy. A family friend hired me to illustrate a card game she had designed for children with a dragon theme. Years later she used the illustrations for her books without ever asking permission or paying me for additional rights. As a graphic designer I became well aware of how easily images can be copied and adapted. As an artist I could see how difficult it could be to make a living, especially in these crazy days on the internet frontier.

When Dragon Tales came out, the characters looked awfully familiar...

Fortunately, my mother and I were able to work out a system that could allow me to continue drawing for her without going broke. As her career grew from writing to public speaking, she would commission drawings from me to use in her presentations.

When she gave me a concept she would talk about the feelings behind it, very passionately, and then let me draw.

Some cute but very un-funny illustrations emerged that got some points across about the stress of parenting, and how family patterns repeat over the years.

Over the years, we developed our own family patterns, but good ones based on her respect for my artistic abilities, and my appreciation for the important work she does in prevention and positive parenting.

We worked hard to learn how to communicate and have good boundaries as collaborators, co-workers, and family.

It takes no more energy to lift someone up

than it does to put them down.

If I'm OK with me,
I have no need
to make you wrong.

Listen to children when they're seven, and they'll talk to you when they're seventeen.

AHA!
YOU'RE BEING
GOOD!

I'd Rather Be Drawing (drawing off the clock)

But it hasn't been all pretty pictures. When you've got something to share with the world it takes a lot of work to package it and market it so it gets out there to people. My mom really needed my help when the publisher of her first book went belly-up. Overnight I became the graphics department of LifeSkills Press, putting all the tricks I'd learned behind the scenes at *The Weekly* to work. The career path I'd never intended turned out to be publishing parenting & self-help books.

It made sense, in that I'd taught my mom everything she knew about parenting... but it sure felt like an odd fit for a rebellious twenty-something fresh out of college, bursting at the seams for adventure and independence...and trying every day of her life NOT to become a parent.

Publishing *The Real World Adventures of Sammy Sperm* and *Emily Egg's Guide to Fashion* (paper doll and coloring books) in my spare time was a natural reaction.

My part-time job with LifeSkills Press designing forms, flyers, and ads allowed me to get a part-time job as a graphic designer in a copy shop designing forms, flyers, and ads.

With two steady day jobs and a part-time illustration/graphic design business, I could spend my nights drawing more radically subversive comics.

Or stapling.

It's a book!

After hours, I used my employee discount to run my underground comics empire. *Sammy Sperm* became a best-seller in underground paper doll book terms.*

*a whopping one hundred and eighty copies! 93

Submit to Authority (getting successfully published)

REAL cartoonists—the ones whose names you know—REAL cartoonists get published in magazines and newspapers. REAL cartoonists get their stuff read; their characters get recognized, and they get paid to draw. REAL cartoonists draw more than one cartoon in a series. REAL cartoonists draw all their cartoons the same size. REAL cartoonists use the same pen name every time...

Self-publishing was fun, and the artistic control is awesome, but every night when I went to bed exhausted from stapling, trimming, or tracking orders, I dreamed of having OTHER people publish my stuff.

To qualify as a REAL cartoonist I learned I had to earn my rejection letter from the New Yorker. (Every REAL cartoonist has one. Some cartoon SUPERSTARS even have acceptance letters.) Then I sent stuff to a bunch of other magazines—starting with the ones who pay the most and working my way down the list— to newspapers, syndicates, literary agents, and other random art markets. Over the years I got a lot of encouragement and even some hand-written rejection letters (which are to be considered good-luck trophies) and encouragement to "keep at it." But nothing really ever "clicked," even though one company wrote me a fat check to re-create my "Relax" cartoon as a polar bear floating in a pool.

I tried not to take it too personally, but after a few years it was hard not to start seeing my submissions as "rejection applications." I saw it as building up my emotional skin in the same way an athlete builds muscle. After all, getting published is an endurance sport.

Dear Kristen, _____ date

We received your submission(s) and
☐ died laughing.
☐ smirked quietly to ourselves.
☐ were simply not amused.

We are ☐ returning them to you.
☐ filing them ☐ in the circular file.
☐ under "top secret."
☐ for future bonfires.
☐ planning to print _____
in our _____ issue. (item)

Please ☐ contact us at _____.
☐ send ☐ a photostat
☐ the original
by _____
(date)

A check for ☐ $1,000,000
☐ $1000
☐ $72.36
☐ _____
will be sent to you on publication.

Yours Truly, _____
editor

94

Fortunately, Bay Area underground newspapers were always happy to publish my special brand of cute weirdness.

Unfortunately, they didn't pay anything. On the contrary, I often ended up volunteering. I also had many enticing opportunities to try not to feel like a token female.

Not my art! Thanks Gary Kell, K. capelli of Grunge & the comical!

95

Indeed, women cartoonists are rare and wonderful beings. (Open the funny papers and see what I mean.) We need one another. I joined an Amateur Publishing Association (APA) of women cartoonists called "Friends of Lulu" (FOL).

In some ways it was not unlike Mills: a place for women to get educated and compare notes on the world they shared.

I took a few copies of *The Reason She Left* to Comicon with FOL (back when it was actually about comics), and shopped it around to publishers. One admired it deeply but told me, "This is great, but it's way ahead of it's time. No one will print it right now. This industry only focuses on fourteen-year-old boys."

Sigh. Thank goodness for shōjo manga, which appeared a decade thereafter and proved that fourteen-year-old girls like comics, too. And a wave of graphic novels followed.

In the olden days before blogs, there were these things called 'zines. In FOL's prehistoric paper forum, and **W**omen **I**n **C**omics and **C**artoon **A**rts, each member would submit a page, and the editor-of-the-month would copy and bind all the pages together and send them out.

I lost touch with all of these amazing and talented cartoonists when I went on to other things. Many of them kept at it and became REAL cartoonists—or at least cartoon professionals.

And FOL continues to guard the interests of girls and women in the cartooning world.

96 Not my art! Thanks Trina Robbins, and Marjorie Henderson Buell!

Supporting the/my Arts (becoming independently wealthy)

As an easily inspired (and distracted) person, I realize now how the cartooning roulette of a world saturated with artists and increasingly unwelcoming to print media wore me out. I also realize how every effort was part of the process of figuring out how to best use my talents. Without total commitment to the business of submissions (binders and postage and logs—oh, my!), or a staff job at a design firm, newspaper, magazine or greeting card company, the life of a cartoonist wasn't panning out to be as glamorous as all that. But I was free (liberal), for the most part, to be able to be creative every day.

My aching dream was always for my art career to be self-sustaining. I longed for each "child of my mind" to be able to go out in the world and support itself—and maybe send a few bucks home to old mom to help with the other kids. I would have happily settled for a patron, like Michelangelo had the Medicis.

I kept thinking about that letter for the Women's Foundation. I needed to do some serious fundraising for myself.

When enough people told me my clever cable-docking device (see Appendage 9) was "a million dollar idea," I decided to put my money where my mouth was. If I could capitalize on bringing this ONE creative idea to the market, I could quit *all* my day jobs and devote *all* my time to the liberal arts!

Astonishingly, I raised $10,000 from friends and family, and gave it to a company to help get me a patent. After two years' work (time I could have spent drawing or writing, of course), and two patent attorneys, however, it became distressingly clear that the design was unpatentable.*

Tail between my legs, I chalked it up to a lesson learned.... If only I'd invested that money in building a talking sperm empire!

Don't be caught cable-diving in front of your clients... get CABLE DOCK™!

*unless I put it on the market first, begging the question.

97

In addition to drawing for free, drawing on the job, drawing *as* a job, drawing off the clock, getting published and becoming independently wealthy, I always was crushingly tempted to pursue my final enticing option:

Give up!

When I saw my beloved pediatrician for the last time before starting college, she asked me what I wanted to do with my life. I told her I wanted to be an artist. Her face fell, and she asked, "Isn't there anything else you could do? It's so hard to make a living as an artist." First my jaw dropped, then I clenched it grimly: I'd show her! But deep down somewhere I believed her. If only she'd said, "If you really have an artistic gift, you have to use it, or you will become apathetic about your life's purpose."

If only every doctor would tell every patient, "Understand and develop your gifts or they will eat away at your mental and physical health. Using them will bring you happiness and health, and the world will be better for it."

I am so lucky (and wise, I think,) to have chosen a partner who believes in creativity, in comedy, and in cartooning. And who has a nine-to-five job with health insurance. Dave's stability has allowed me to be an entrepreneur and stay home with our son...and listen to my muses.

And they never shut up.

So I'll never give up.

8

presenting:

Inside the Mills Revolution

And now we return to Mills.

Mills College: "Not a girl's school without men," as a favorite t-shirt says, "but a women's college without boys." Two years after I'd graduated, Mills almost had to get a new slogan. In May of 1990, I accompanied my mother to a conference in Phoenix where she was a keynote speaker. I sold and signed books at her conference table. I was bored out of my mind.

That afternoon, we passed a newsstand and saw a sea of Mills women crying on all the front pages. I was stunned to read the news, which explained the board's decision to go coed. "Buncha whiners," the photo captions implied.

That night as I walked around the rim of the Grand Canyon, I marveled at the quiet depths of nature's wonders, but my heart was broken at the loss of a special place in the world. My life had moved on, but the memory of my time at Mills (the frogs, the eucalyptus, the keen challenges and gifts of a community of only women) was still fresh in my mind. The full moon must have been throbbing with "woman energy" that night, for I felt called back to my alma mater. When I arrived on campus, the the emotional outburst had turned into action. The strike was well-organized and in full swing. There was nothing for me to do but wander around and draw what I saw.

What I saw was the entire alumnae association siding with the students. Women's college communities everywhere also stuck up for their sister. Elsewhere, people mocked those wailing women. But on campus, they were no longer crying. They were running a peaceful strike.

Without the internet, without email, without cell phones, their communication channels were clear. The snowflake-like glyphs you'll see in the story represent their impressive and patient process. Watch the news today. You'll rarely see a strike or demonstration done this right. History continues to demonstrate how right these young, upfront feminists got it: they had a clearly stated goal (reverse the decision!) and found a way to make it happen. Both sides worked together to solve a problem, as it should be in any caring community of learners, neighbors, or citizens.

The next 16 pages contain the reprint of my 1990 comic book. Imagine a bright yellow cover...

Those Mills girls were 'perfectly revolting!'

BANNED
from Campus Bookstore

inside the

Mills

Revolution

a cartoon history
by Kristen Baumgardner

In the academic year of 1989-90, Mills College began an intensive self-survey to determine its strengths and weaknesses and help to position it as an independent Liberal Arts college entering the 21st century.

It was determined that the college would need to increase enrollment in order to compete with comparable institutions and maintain its health in the long run. As it has in single-sex institutions since women first demanded public education, the debate arose whether to go coed. Mary Metz, the president of Mills and a figurehead of cheerful self-composure and perfect hair, invited debate from all sectors of the community. Although almost everyone felt Mills was in need of some change, most did not believe the coed option was to be taken seriously.

Three weeks before graduation, the fate of the college was to be revealed. Astonishing the entire community, Chairman of the Board Warren Hellman announced that men would be admitted as undergraduates at Mills in the fall of 1990. The response was a wail heard 'round the world. It was the voice of outrage at the betrayal of Mills' 138-year history and commitment as an institution for women's education. The Board's decision showed little faith in Mills' identity and potential. The students shut the campus down, blocking entry to every administrative office, and "politely requested" that the decision be reversed.

The strike attracted the attention of the national media, which sparked debates throughout the country on women's education, sexism, and the nebulous state of the women's movement. On campus, the level of organization was remarkable. Decisions were made by consensus, with runners from each blockaded doorway meeting again and again at headquarters until the entire campus was in agreement. One alumna provided walkie talkies that made spontaneous action possible. One night, for example, when a secret meeting was called at the President's house, cars were called from all over campus to "honk it out," making so much noise that communication within was impossible.

The entire community mobilized to show its commitment. Within ten days the Alumnae Association had raised hundreds of thousands of dollars to keep Mills a women's college. The trustees were presented with proposals from every quarter of the community to meet its needs and goals without "selling out."

Images appeared and repeated. One strike T-shirt played on the timeless Mills motto: "Remember who you are and what you represent." It read, "The students remembered, the staff remembered, the faculty remembered, the alumni remembered...the administration forgot."

The rest, of course, is "herstory." After a two-week siege, the Board reversed the decision and blockaders went home to take showers. This is the eyewitness journal of the strike by a roving cartoonist who started her career at Mills.

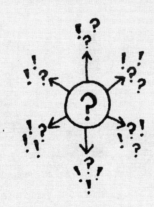

105

108

And in the End...

Mills College is in a state of renewal and revitalization; outreach programs and curriculum changes reflect Mills' commitment to growth and change. A renewed commitment to posters and witty, succinct slogans, for example, led to an exciting billboard advertising Mills to San Francisco commuters. Men of Mills College t-shirts and totes hit the market.

Fifteen minutes of fame put Mills on the map; now whenever its name is mentioned it sparks a debate on women's education (although unsolicited opinions, thank goodness, do not come as forcefully or as frequently as they did that fateful week in May). The revolution at Mills gave hope to other women's colleges facing similar struggles, and Mills itself continues to be a forum for - and a leader in - the education of women of all ages, from all backgrounds.

PROUD WOMEN.
STRONG WOMEN.
MILLS WOMEN.

ALL WOMEN.

Mary Metz resigned over the summer (presumably from the shock of seeing these cartoons), without the author ever having had a chance to affectionately tousle her hair. Some bald students grew their hair back, others kept the look and set new fashion trends in the Bay Area.

P.S. This cartoon journal won a first place prize in the 1990 Bay Guardian cartoon contest, catapulting its author into a glamorous international career.

David Letterman's Top Ten Reasons
Mills College Coeds Didn't Want Men Admitted:

10. No more going to the library topless.

9. Amateur production of Checkov's "Three Sisters" replaced by three-day "Stooge-A-Thon."

8. Football team has perfect 0-452 record.

7. Guys often whoop and holler when words like "breast" appear in sensitive poetry.

6. There's going to be some loser named Ned who keeps asking everyone out.

5. They might try to free the men we use in our science projects.

4. We're shy.

3. Afraid cafeteria walls might be covered with "Dukes of Hazzard" posters.

2. Less beer for the rest of us.

1. They tend to spit a lot.

We had a revolution.
There was childcare,
there was consensus,
we sent thank you notes,
we cleaned up after ourselves,
and we won.
We won!

A few months after the strike, I walked into the campus bookstore with a stomach full of butterflies and an arm-full of my bright-yellow *Inside the Mills Revolution* booklets. I walked out of there a publisher, a grown-up, self-directed Mills Woman, with a consignment contract in my hand.

That night, I received a call from the public relations office at Mills. A woman from with whom I had occasionally worked as a work-study illustrator and graphic designer was calling. At first I was delighted when she mentioned having seen my books in the store, and hoped she was calling to help support my efforts on Mills' behalf. But the tone of her voice was not at all cheerful. My cartoons had made personal attacks on the president! She said she was ashamed of me—a formerly upstanding and promising student. But...but...but.... I won an award for the cartoon collection, I tried to say. I had actually always liked the president, I tried to say. It's nothing personal, I tried to say.

The remarkable thing about the student strike, especially in light of other recent political protests, was a mutual respect on both sides. The trustees never called the police or criminalized the students; they simply challenged the strikers to rise to the occasion and help solve the problem (which they did with financial commitments from the alumnae). On the students' part, there was a notable lack of name-calling. I had to search hard for a symbol of Metz's "evilness" to convey the anger and betrayal students felt toward her—finally settling on her perfect hair. The worst that people called her (that I heard) was "The Georgia Peach."

Our president had been a nice lady who represented a certain character germane to Mills since the eighteen-hundreds. An aura of businesslike politeness pervaded Mills when I was there, and can still be found in some classes where students do what is asked of them but don't speak up, challenge or provoke. Still, when it came down to it, the students proved that a women's education really does is give women permission to turn social graces into social action. And when nice girls mean business...they get results.

Of course, I couldn't verbalize any of this on the phone to a very tense and upset person who was now raising her voice at me. Emotions on campus were still raw. No one on the striking side had the perspective yet to see what an important role Metz had played in galvanizing the community to re-commit to its values, even at the expense of her own public trust. At the time of the phone call she was still the president, and had not yet made her graceful and ladylike exit.

The P.R. lady told me I couldn't sell my books on campus, and to come pick them up. I was stunned. I hung up the phone and wept with disappointment and outrage, in true Mills Woman fashion. So much for my business. So much for my cartooning career. So much for the extra month's rent I'd sunk into printing. Back to Top Ramen and popcorn. The box of books would have to be re-purposed as an end-table in my rented room. Edgy political cartoons, I learned once again, was not welcome at Mills.

I called a girlfriend to share my sob story, and her husband answered the phone. I told him my sad story. He laughed at me. "So your first book was banned," he said. "What an honor! That must mean it's great! Think of the company it's in!"

I hung up and went to my computer. I designed a "Banned" sticker to make myself feel better, and vowed not to give up. By the time I picked up my stock from Mills, my banned book was on the racks in three San Francisco bookstores and one in Oakland, and I had been invited to speak on a panel about Women in Cartooning.

And a month later it was back in the campus bookstore. Mary Metz had resigned. It sold like hotcakes, and so did the Men of Mills College t-shirts and totebags. I bought some sandwiches.

A year later I got a call from the Women's Museum in Dallas, Texas, asking permission to hang a cartoon from this collection in the permanent timeline representing the strike, which apparently made history beyond the gates of Mills. I was speechless! (Thank goodness they didn't ask me to give a speech.)

Staples on the few remaining copies of *Inside the Mills Revolution* from that printing twenty years ago may have long since rusted through. The slim books may have been stained with coffee, lost in shuffles, tossed in the trash or, hopefully, recycled. But one panel was given a special job, and would help keep the story of these brave, whiney, hysterical women alive beyond the gates of Mills and into the future. (And by hysterical I mean both distressed *and* funny.) (As a matter of fact, the Latin word for "womb" is *hyster*, so by definition anything a human with a uterus does is *hyster*ical...and/or *hystor*ical...but that's another book.)

I felt proud to have played a small part in this small story in the big picture of women's education, where we can find our wisdom...power...balance...confidence...cuteness.... All rolled together in one.

Women in a Jeep!

Bonus cartoon & commentary in Appendage 10.

Epilogue

I didn't realize at the time that I was drawing my last cartoon. A year passed between the idea and the sketch, another between the sketch and the ink, and fifteen more flew by before the pencil lines were erased. I found this character in a notebook while I was scanning all of my Mills cartoons.

She's my idol.

This lady is a souvenir from the days when I first would hear people use the term "Renaissance Man"—the enlightened guy who does everything—and think, "Why doesn't anyone ever say 'Renaissance Woman?'" But now people do. It also struck me funny that "Renaissance Man" might have been, say, Ben Franklin's secret superhero identity.

If I were a superhero, I'd be too nerdy to hang out with Spiderman or Batman. I probably wouldn't fight over-the-top bad guys in building-busting battles and butt-kicking ballets. No, I would rather be someone who fought ignorance with science, art, and poetry. Like Marie Curie. Or Maya Angelou. I would be all my muses rolled into one.

Yeah, Renaissance Woman is the one who shows up after the battles and says, "Hey guys, let's clean this mess up." She teaches people new skills and cheers them up with her positive attitude. She says "bullshit" to power-tripping bullies and helpless victims alike, and uses her incredible crystal magnetism to comfort the fearful and get them to listen to reason. She can sail a ship, construct a building, and teach a new language in a single bound, through the powers of enthusiasm, humor, and politeness.

Why did I stop drawing cartoons? Because I got too busy. After Dave moved in I started spending my spare time balancing my checkbook and shopping for tablecloths and toilet paper. No longer able to leave scraps of paper laying around the living room for days, I packed up the pens and exacto knives to make room for finger paints and crayons. I downsized my creative life into a miniature P.C. the size of a book—which opened up a new world of words.

But there's another reason. Maybe Renaissance Woman was the last thing I drew because in her I found, in some way, what I had been seeking.

I'm still learning how to knit.

If I were a superhero, I'd be

"RENAISSANCE WOMAN"

wisdom of the ages belongs to her

Light of Reason to guide humanity through times of darkness

paisley is the oldest design; shaped like a sperm or a fetus; she wears power in her hair

lovely manners

not necessarily a blond

cool jewelry to remember that slavery is no fun

strong, white teeth (yes, she bites)

knowledge of good and evil? "So I said, 'Give me a bite!'"

wields a pen AND a sword

she can't fly but will walk bravely through all kinds of weather

can knit a sweater in minutes flat

hammers in the morning, in the evening, all over this land

able to navigate her way out of any situation; natural laws her allies

plays all instruments (but a harmonica fits here better than a steel drum)

a healer by all methods that work

knees: do not jerk

(hard to leap tall buildings and fixed societal structures in high heels)

stands firmly on the ground; walks lightly on the earth

Appendages

1. Women Who Made History
How many did you get right? (How many did *I* get right?)

Marie Curie
Katherine Hepburn
Margaret Thatcher
Alice Walker

Eleanor Roosevelt
Benazir Bhutto
Geraldine Ferraro
Babe Didrickson-Zaharias

Indira Gandhi
Georgia O'Keefe
Sojurner Truth
Delores Huerta

Jeanne Wakatsuki Houston
Zora Neale Hurston
Margaret Mead
Lily Tomlin

Bonus: Personal History

My Last Boss
My Grandma
My Mom
My Artsy Bad Young Self

2. Map O' Mills

when I drove the van

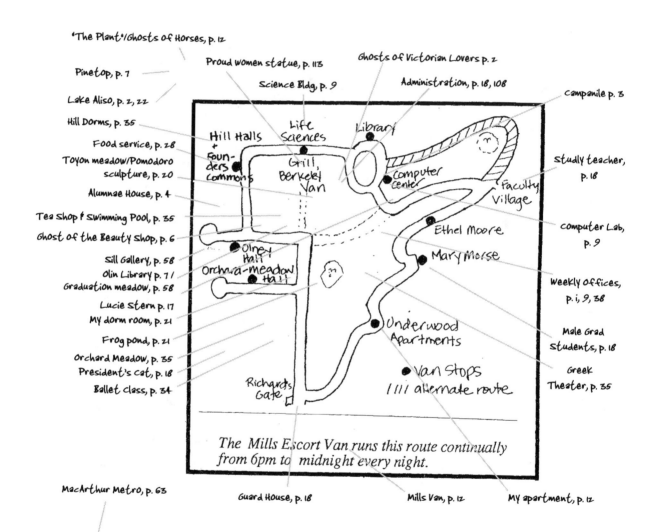

'The Plant'/Ghosts of Horses, p. 12

Pinetop, p. 7

Lake Aliso, p. 2, 22

Hill Dorms, p. 35

Food service, p. 28

Toyon meadow/Pomodoro
sculpture, p. 20

Alumnae House, p. 4

Tea Shop & Swimming Pool, p. 35

Ghost of the Beauty Shop, p. 6

Sill Gallery, p. 58

Olin Library p. 7 /
Graduation meadow, p. 58

Lucie Stern p. 17

My dorm room, p. 21

Frog pond, p. 21

Orchard Meadow, p. 35

President's cat, p. 18

Ballet class, p. 34

Proud women statue, p. 113

Science Bldg, p. 9

Ghosts of Victorian Lovers p. 2

Administration, p. 18, 108

Campanile p. 3

Studly teacher, p. 18

Faculty Village

Computer Lab, p. 9

Ethel Moore

Mary Morse

Weekly Offices, p. i, 9, 38

Underwood Apartments

Male Grad Students, p. 18

Greek Theater, p. 35

Van Stops

//// alternate route

Hill Halls & Founders Commons

Life Sciences

Grill, Berkeley Van

Library

Computer Center

Olney Hall

Orchard-Meadow Hall

Richards Gate

The Mills Escort Van runs this route continually from 6pm to midnight every night.

MacArthur Metro, p. 63

Guard House, p. 18

Mills Van, p. 12

My apartment, p. 12

The World Outside, p. 57

126

3. "Safe Love"
a song for the emotionally insecure redneck

Letters to the Editor

The Weekly welcomes letters to the editor. All letters must be turned in by the Monday preceding the Friday issue. Letters can be turned in to the Weekly office or the Weekly box in Mills Hall

Swim-A-Thon a big success

Editors: Thanks to all who supported the Mills swim team, Swim-a-Thon. Through your generosity, the team will be able to fly to their championship meet in Long Beach, California on February 18, 19, and 20th.

---The Mills College swim team: Amy Council, Cheryl Laton, Christine Hatch, Colleen Kinney, Jeannette Moore, Jenny Lentz, Karen Koshak, Keri Sweet and Melissa Noble

Ode to Racism

Editors: Lately there has been a resurgence of racist incidents on college and university campuses. It is ironical that such attitudes of racism should occur in places of learning.

Your first editorial on "Perspectives" offers hope that the *Weekly* will work to help sensitize and educate Mills students, faculty and administrators about the diversity of out multicultural society, thus promoting unity.

ODE TO RACISM

There are two things that bother me, so please

explain them if you can. Why do white people think

that all black people are alike?

Why are we classed by color first?

I don't know which assumption is worse —

both are a downright shame

Why can't we be judged by our character and name?

Is this another missing piece of the puzzle of life? What an unfair game.

---A BLACK WOMENS COLLECTIVE BOOSTER

Racist cartoon?

Editors: I really enjoy reading the Weekly and look forward to its publication each Friday.

I did not, however, appreciate the racial overtone depicted on the last weeks cartoon. We are all aware that the majority of janitors and groundsmen on this campus are ethnic minorities (which in itself says a lot about Mills), but they do not wear marijuana plants in their uniforms, and to portray them as doing so is stereotyping.

I agree that they choose some inopportune moments to run their blowers, lawn mowers etc. but overall they do a great job of keeping this campus clean and well groomed. To associate them with drugs based on their race is unfair so please stay away from stereotyping and continue to produce a well written, professional paper.

---Alicia Allums

in reference to the crew team in the "Men of Mills" cartoon...

REBUTTAL

The crew team has taken a poll and none of us consider ourselves to be bull dykes.

What the hell is a bull dyke anyway?

As opposed to a cow dyke? We don't have any of those either.

But we do consider ourselves to be...

* happy
* strong
* intelligent
* healthy
* energetic
* creative
* competitive
* funny
* open minded
* spontaneous
* special
* tough
* and generally a cool bunch of people.

(P.S. NO ARGUMENT HERE! love, the offending cartoonist)

Sincerely, The Mills College Crew Team

Ed Co

From Co

what we a going to g American come a little a little more my word for pers. Talk to p. Look for infor the mainstrea... media (try *The Nation*). And ask questions. Ask all the questions you want. Because somebody has to start making the American government accountable for what they are doing in Nicaragua, and that somebody is you.

L.J. Hedges

:::::::::::::::::::
CORRECTIONS
The poem printed last week in the poetry corner on page 10 was inadvertently not attributed. We definitely want to give the author credit for a fine poem. The poet's name is **BETSY ALLBRIGHT**. Sorry for the mistake!
:::::::::::::::::::

Editors: I found last week's comic, "Men of Mills" humorless and offensive. The comic displays a lack of taste. It is obvious that the artist pointed out certain people. Comics like these question the need for censorship, since the cartoonist shows little restraint and respect for others.

I found this comic to be below Mills Weekly standards.

— **Name Withheld**

5. More Turkey Talk
holiday bonus cartoon

MORE TURKEY TALK:

Did You Know:

Turkeys are

SO

DUMB...

that they can't

stay out in the rain!

"Why," you ask?

Because: **THEY DROWN INSTANTLY!**

intense.

wow.

--BELIEVE IT
...or don't.

baumgardnes. 11/20.

Now: consider the saying:

YOU ARE

duh...

WHAT
YOU
EAT.

...and more fun with forks!

POLLY PILGRIM SAYS:

"The most beautiful color in the world is half yam and half cranberry sauce. Try it this Thanksgiving!"

God bless this mess...

Bad press, I know... but hey, if it works...

Boycott Inhumane Holidays!

6. The Van Ness Monster

© 1991 by Gary Kell

Little-known San Francisco legends: the only known photo of the **Van Ness Monster**

7. Non-Toxic Cleaners
kid-friendly — designed for a pre-school!

MEET THE INGREDIENTS...

Hi, we're plain old liquid soap.
Regular dishsoap or Dr. Bronner's. Use us with water
for washing dishes and mopping the floor—no need to
buy toxic cleaners! If you want bubbles, add water to
soap. If you don't want bubbles, add soap to water.

(alkaline ph)

(I'm a Sponge)

(alkaline ph)

Hi, I'm Baking Soda.
I'm THE best natural scrubber for soap scum and gunk. Keep
me in a shaker jar (think parmesan cheese) by your sink to
sprinkle on pots and pans. Spray with Cleaning Spray and let
sit while you're having dinner... then wipe clean!

Hi, I'm Tea Tree Oil.
I'm a natural antiseptic and Australia's favorite germ-
killer. Keep me handy in your medicine cabinet for pimples
and bug-bites, and add me to your cleaners!

MIX THE CLEANERS...

All-Purpose Cleaning Spray
Made with 3 Tbsp. liquid soap and water. Soap and water get
most of the germs—and ALL of the dirt! Use everywhere.
Add 10-20 drops scented oil if desired.

(alkaline ph)

Disinfencting Cleaning Spray (alkaline ph.)
Add 20-30 drops of Tea Trea Oil to the
All-Purpose Cleaning Spray to kill the rest
of the germs. Great for bathrooms!

Squeaky Cleaning Spray
Mix half vinegar and half water in a squirt bottle (add
10-20 drops peppermint oil or tea-trea oil to boost cleaning power and mask the "pickle" smell). Great for floors
and neutralizing soap sprays

(acid ph)

8. Homemade Hybrids
Some things just make me want to BLOG!

My biggest pet peeve (other than towns and cities that don't offer recycling programs) is how mindlessly Americans idle their engines. After watching *An Inconvenient Truth* I went on a mission to find out the truth about how many seconds or minutes of gas are actually used when you start your car. What I discovered surprised me! Think about it: idling (going nowhere with the motor running) gets exactly ZERO miles per gallon. Between global warming, gas prices and oil wars, it just doesn't make sense to use fuel for anything other than motion.

Even though debates rage about ignition wear vs. engine wear, auto mechanics agree that today's engines don't use much gas to start up, and there is no need to warm up a cold engine before you drive.

Many cities around the world have found that no-idling zones make a difference (especially around schools), and the Lung Association agrees. At a time when every little bit counts, make a little bit of difference. Kill your engine when you pull over to use your phone, order a meal, talk to a friend, or drop off kids. If traffic's like a parking lot, then park until it starts moving! Little differenes add up to a lot. So, **"all in favor of saving gas, raise your right foot!"** THANK YOU!

CUT EMISSIONS RIGHT NOW WITH THE

10 SECOND RULE

Did you know that:

- It only takes ten seconds worth of gas to start a warm engine.

- Kicking the idling habit can get you 10-20% more miles on a tank of gas.

- Every gallon of gas saved keeps 25 lbs of CO2 out of the atmosphere.

Find out more, download free materials, and talk about it at **homemadehybrid.blogspot.com**

Until I can afford a real one, I'm driving a

HOMEMADE HYBRID

BREAK THE IDLING HABIT - CLEAR THE AIR

© 2008 K CAVEN

homemadehybrid.blogspot.com

9. The Cable Dock

"a million-dollar idea"

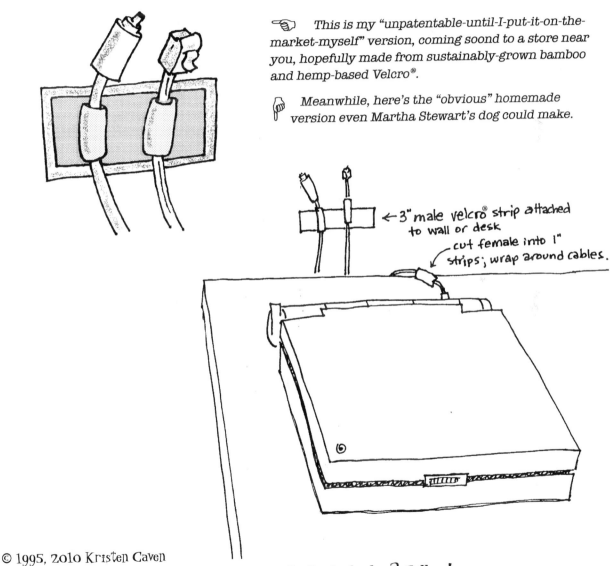

☞ This is my "unpatentable-until-I-put-it-on-the-market-myself" version, coming soon to a store near you, hopefully made from sustainably-grown bamboo and hemp-based Velcro®.

☞ Meanwhile, here's the "obvious" homemade version even Martha Stewart's dog could make.

← 3" male velcro® strip attached to wall or desk

cut female into 1" strips; wrap around cables.

Patent pending time and energy. Know anyone in the doo-hicky biz? Call me!

10. SPAM
is bad and evil

In recent years, "SPAM" has become a slogan for students at Mills:

Strong Women
Proud Women
All Women
Mills Women.

Which is unfortunate.

Not only because SPAM is evil (both the canned processed mystery meat AND the emails that ruined the internet for all of us), but because in 1990, Mills Women stood strong and proud... with love and hope for ALL WOMEN of the world.

About the Author

Doctor, I Think I Have a Muse

by Kristen Caven

One of the reasons Kristen chose to complete her education at Mills College is because they allow students to design their own major. Thanks to this program, Kristen may be the only person you know who has a degree in *Myth and the Western Mind*. She continues to enjoy the freedom of thought that her education allows her, and wishes this *liber*-ty for all people.

Kristen's two greatest personal challenges are 1) balancing her desire to help others with the demands of her own creative impulses and 2) balancing the demands of her own creative impulses with the demands of her own creative impulses. She has recently come to accept the fact that she will never be able to write all the books she wants to, and must settle for designing their covers.

Kristen's only regret at Mills is that some tired but well-meaning volunteer mis-typed her favorite quote in the Mills College yearbook. (Her picture would have been plenty dorky enough next to elegant writing that made poetic sense.) She has discovered that in real life, glamour is as elusive as time to draw cartoons.

Plagued By Muses

by Kristen Caven

Kristen Baumgardner
Myth and the Western Mind
Perhaps the mission of all mankind is to make people laugh at the truth, to make people laugh . . . because the only truth lies in learning to free ourselves from an insane passion for the truth.
— William of Baskerville
in the Name of the Rose by Umberto Eco

THE TRUTH

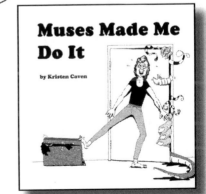

Muses Made Me Do It

by Kristen Caven

Keep up with Kristen on her website, www.kristencaven.com.

Attributions

(3-7, 11-23, 27-46, 59) printed in *The Weekly* 1987-1988

(7) Life in Hell rabbit © Matt Groening

(8, 125) images © their subjects; photographers unknown

(31, 36) illustrations from The *Winning Family* by Louise Hart, Ed.D.

(30, 31, 90, 91) illustrations for Louise Hart www.drlouisehart.com

(49) drawn in collaboration with Brian Lee. Logo © The Kido Institute.

(58) card by Suzy Becker of Suzy's Zoo, www.suzybecker.com

(70) cartoon by Gail Machlis, www.artalchemy.biz

(84) Jim Pryatel

(87) Sketches from French Lessons program by Michelle Bennett

(88) illustration from *Answering God's Call* by Roberta Lynch, and *Taming Your Dragons* (and *Taming Your Dragons*, and *Stress Relief for Kids: Taming Your Dragons*) by Martha Belknap

(95, 130) cover of *The Comical &* Van Ness Monster by Gary Kell

(95) K. Capelli, cover of *Grunge*

(96) artwork © Trina Robbins for **Friends of Lulu** & **W.I.C.C.A**. www.trinarobbins.com

(112) Lyrics © Tracy Chapman

(113, 126, 134) based on *Strong Women, Proud Women* logo & *Power of Woman* sculpture by Roberta Weir, www.weirgallery.com

(115) © David Letterman and NBC, reprinted with permission

(116) quote by Heather Cox, www.coxart.com

(131) adapted from *Clean and Green* by Annie Berthold-Bond

(137) Umberto Eco , *The Name of the Rose,* http://umbertoeco.com

An economy-sized thank you to Dave and Donald for all the help and funny bits and laughter and scanning and encouragement and love and support and Guitar Hero — you ROCK!

More thanks to my awesomely helpful readers: Paige, Stephanie, Neepa and Dave, Ann and Mom... and to Steven for help down the home stretch... and to Linda Jasquez-Fiorri and the AAMC and everyone at Mills for the warm embrace.

Dear...

Damian (vi, 112), Shari (vi), Rhonda (vi, 56), Dave (vi, 33, 42, 78, 98, 144), Jack Lincoln (vi, 50), Athena, Clover, etc. (2), Christina Smith (4, 38), Jennifer Nichols, Tamara Tucker (4), Jan Miner (6), Penny, Suzette, Moya and the gang (7), Steve Jobs (10, 87), Gary Larson (11), Rick Gray (16, 40, 51, 83) Elizabeth Siekhaus (16), All the Men of Mills (you know who you are -- but especially Eric Sanford) and Annie Stenzel (18), Bruce Pavlik (21), Kilian Melloy (22), Walt Disney (24) Mom, a.k.a. Louise Hart, Ed.D. (26, 89, 142), William Shakespeare (42, 43), Jesus of Nazareth (44), Trina Robbins (*A Century of Women Cartoonists*) (48), Brian Lee (49), Barb Roseman (52-54, 134), Margie (56, 65), Valerie Guth, Suzy Becker, Barry Gantt (the most glamorous cartoonist of all), (58), Tony Murphy, Gary Kell, Glenn Gulmes & the Comical Gang (64, 95), All my Deco Dames & Dons (you know who you are — but especially Laurie, Sara, Alexa, Theresa, Margie, Paul, Raul) (65), Mr. Rick (67), Bette Davis & Joe Mankiewicz (68), Gail "She called to say she's in love...with an idea" Machlis (70), William/Bill Mize (71), Aristophanes (*Lysistrata*) with a shout-out to Kathryn Blume (*Operation Lysistrata, The Boycott*) (73), Nick Kazetc. (74), Paul Scherman (86), Copy Central gang & Bookpeople gang (93), Trina Robbins, Nina Paley, Joan Hilty and Cheela Smith my buds (96), Mills Students & Alumnae, Mary Metz, Warren Hellman (100-118), Uncle Rich, Aunt Vicki, Aunt Rita, Uncle Mel, and Mom (109), Heather Cox (56, 116, 128), Sandy Israel (117), Dad (132), Caitlin Ayers (134), Pat Palmer, Maddy (142), Jenny Flynn Israel (144)...

...my Muses Love You!

Thanks for your inspiration.

STANDING OVULATION

Other Books the Author Wrote...

RETURNING TO PRINT IN 2011

A Match Made in Utero

A double-duty gender-education paper doll and coloring book!

Sammy and Emily are together forever (AND different but perfectly equal in every way) in this double-direction paper doll coloring book. Contains Sammy Sperm's Real World Adventures on one side and Emily Egg's Guide to Fashion on the other. Also contains Sammy & Emily's guides to safe and unsafe sex, plus Shakesperm Theater.

"These are not your Dover paper dolls."
— Alstair, Bookseller

Emily Egg's FairyGoddessAngel-Priestess Newage Coloring and Reading Book

A guide to female deities as personified by Emily Egg, with super-retro Newage appeal. you already know the *Tooth Fairy* and the *Angel of Fortune*. Meet the *Goddess of Parking and Traffic* (shaped like a tire, of course), the *Angel of Shoes*, and the *High Priestess of Stuff*.

"We fell out of our chairs laughing."
— Lisa, Book distributor

The Reason She Left

and Other Stories

Kristen's full-length philosophical comic book/graphic novel about Nettie's odyssey of personal growth is in the company of all of her full-page comics. Stories include *History of the Atomic Theory (chapter one), In God's Country, Not Exactly a Fairy Tale,* and *Ego Sum.*

"A delightful comic— one of the finds of the issue. Full of post-modernism, explanations of new ways of thought, cool young women, thinking people, rationality and intuition."
— R. Seth Friedman,
Factsheet Five

On the Wings of Self-Esteem

By Kristen's lifelong mother and collaborator, Louise Hart, Ed.D., with Kristen as editor/co-writer & illustrator. A guide to recovering lost self-esteem, or finding it in the first place.

"A wonderful book! If everyone in America read this book and did the recommended exercises, half of all the pain and suffering we currently experience would disappear."
— Jack Canfield, author of
Chicken Soup for the Soul

Books The Author Dreams of Writing...

Read **The Winning Family** by Dr. Louise Hart (co-written by Kristen) if you want to learn how to break out of difficult or dysfunctional family patterns, and create a family where everyone feels at home. ☞ **www.drlouisehart.com**

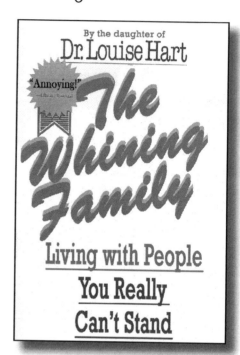

Read **The Whining Family** if you prefer to complain about it for the rest of your life. ☞

☝ Dr. Pat Palmer's classic is great to read to children if you want to improve their self-esteem and build social and emotional literacy. **www.upliftpress.com**

My version is also useful for dogs and cats. ☞

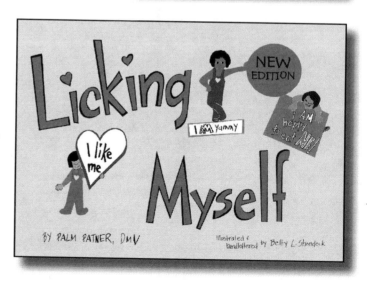

142

Stuff You Can Get....

Many of Kristen's cartoons (and Dave's, too) are available as notecards, postcards, t-shirts, stamps, totebags, and mugs.

RELAX
for anywhere and anytime there is a need to combat stress with laughter or otherwise.

Ostrich Wedding
inside reads *"May Your Necks and Hearts Forever Intertwingle"* —*Ancient Ostrich Wedding Blessing.* Available in all available gender variations.

Men of Mills College
Tote bag, t-shirt, and poster

Renaissance Woman
Poster and apron

And much, much more!

visit www.kristencaven.com

And yes, I take requests!

my hungry typewriter

Book design by Kristen Caven

printed somewhere in interspace

The text of this book is set in 10-point American Typewriter.

Display font: Spumoni

Made in the USA
Charleston, SC
30 April 2010